About the Author

Fergus O'Connell is one of the world's leading authorities on project management and getting things done in the shortest possible time. The *Sunday Business Post* has described him as having 'more strings to his bow than a Stradivarius'. He has a First in Mathematical Physics and has worked in information technology, software development and general management.

Fergus has spent much of the last thirty years either doing, teaching, learning, writing or thinking about project management. In 1992, he founded ETP (www.etpint.com), which is now one of the world's leading programme and project management companies. His project management method – Structured Project Management/The Ten Steps – has influenced a generation of project managers. In 2003 this method was used to plan and execute the Special Olympics World Games 2003, the world's biggest sporting event that year. His radical methods for shortening projects are in use by a growing band of devotees. His experience covers projects around the world; he has taught project management in Europe, North America, South America and the Far East. He holds two patents.

Fergus is the author of eight books, both fiction and non-fiction: *How To Run Successful Projects – The Silver Bullet* (3rd edition, 2001), *How To Run Successful High-Tech Project-Based Organizations* (1999), *How To Run Successful Projects In Web-Time* (2000), *Simply Brilliant – The Competitive Advantage of Common Sense* (2nd edition, 2004), *Call The Swallow* (2002), *How To Do A Great Job – And Go Home On Time* (2005), *Fast Projects: Project Management When Time Is Short* (2007), *How To Get More Done: Seven Days to Achieving More* (2007).

The first of these, sometimes known simply as *The Silver Bullet* has become both a bestseller and a classic. *Simply Brilliant* – also a bestseller –

was runner-up in the W H Smith Book Awards 2002. *Call The Swallow* was shortlisted for the 2002 Kerry Ingredients Irish Fiction Prize and nominated for the Hughes & Hughes/*Sunday Independent* Novel of the Year. His books have been translated into thirteen languages.

Fergus has written on project management for the *Sunday Business Post*, *Computer Weekly* and the *Wall Street Journal*. He has lectured on project management at University College Cork, Trinity College Dublin, Bentley College, Boston University, the Michael Smurfit Graduate School of Business and on television for the National Technological University.

He has two children and lives with his wife in France.

WORK LESS, ACHIEVE MORE

Great Ideas to Get
Your Life Back

Fergus O'Connell

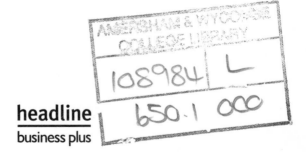

headline
business plus

First published in 2009 by
HEADLINE PUBLISHING GROUP

1

Cataloguing in Publication Data is available from the British Library

ISBN 978 0 7553 1867 4

Typeset in Legato by Susie Bell, susie@f-12.co.uk

Printed and bound in Great Britain by
CPI Mackays, Chatham, ME5 8TD

Headline's policy is to use papers that are natural, renewable and recyclable products and
made from wood grown in sustainable forests. The logging and manufacturing processes are
expected to conform to the environmental regulations of the country of origin.

HEADLINE PUBLISHING GROUP
An Hachette Livre UK Company
338 Euston Road
London NW1 3BH

www.headline.co.uk
www.hachettelivre.co.uk

Dedication

This book is dedicated to you, the reader, in the hope
that it will have a positive impact on your life

Acknowledgements

In a sense this book is the result of the collaboration of thousands of
people. These are the people whom I've been able to work with over the
last twenty years teaching and applying these ideas. If you've ever taught
you'll know that every time you do so you learn something new.
So it has been with me. These people have taught me all that
I have now brought together in this book.

I'd particularly like to thank Garrett Ahearne, Deirdre Fitzgerald, Laura
Grant, Frank Friel, Raymond Smyth and Ciara Chambers. John Moseley,
my publisher at Headline, was the best of co-pilots on this book.
My agent Darin Jewell did a stalwart job throughout.

Contents

Preface

One winter I had an early meeting in Dublin. The meeting was set for 7.30 a.m. and I was staying out in the suburbs. Dublin traffic has become pretty notorious over the last ten years and so I set off early to make sure I wasn't late. As it turned out I overcompensated and arrived in central Dublin just before seven.

It was a horrible morning – pouring rain and with a high wind. It was the kind of weather where an umbrella isn't going to do you any good. The rain will be blowing in from the side and your clothes will be wet before you know it. I parked in one of the city's Georgian squares and sat listening to the radio, killing time until my meeting.

A few minutes after I arrived, a light went on in the basement of one of the buildings. Shortly after that a car pulled up. A man got out as the rain lashed him. He opened the rear door and, reaching in, took out a bundle, shielded with a coat. It was clearly a small child and he hurried his bundle out of the car and down the steps to what, it turned out, was a playschool or crèche. Moments later a woman got out of the car and followed him down with a second bundle.

I suddenly realised that what was going on was nothing more than the kids being dropped off for their day at playschool.

For the rest of that day and ever since then I have often found myself thinking about that family. Simple questions: What time were they all up at so that they could get their kids there at that time? What time would the kids be collected that evening? And what time would they be home? And have eaten? And eaten what? And gone to bed? How much time would they have spent with each other that day? And how were the four of them when the weekend came? Exhausted? Happy? Relieved?

And more profound questions: Were the parents happy doing these things? Was this what they really wanted to do with their lives? And what would the kids remember of their childhood? What would the parents remember of the kids' childhood? And was this the way life has to be in the twenty-first century?

I was reminded of the widely known quote by Thoreau, the American philosopher: 'Most men live lives of quiet desperation.' Whenever I thought of this family I remembered this quote. I found myself wondering whether it was accurate or just something that had passed into the collective consciousness. Eventually, one day, I tracked it down and found what Thoreau actually said. 'Most men live lives of quiet desperation and go to the grave with the song still in them.' It sent – and still sends – a chill down my spine.

It is for this family, and all similar families, that I have written this book.

Introduction

It is possible to spend less time in work and do at least as good and – almost certainly – a better job. If you're a manager you can do this and achieve better business performance from your organisation. Outside of work, it is possible to spend more time on the things you really want to spend time on. You can go to work each day and not feel oppressed by the weight of things you have to do. You can work solid, enjoyable days and leave at a reasonable hour. You can have far more time in your life for the things that really matter to you. This is the essence of *Work Less, Achieve More*. If these ideas appeal to you then you've come to the right place.

You may have tried other books, methods or techniques which claimed or promised to do the same thing. You may have attended expensive training courses or bought classy-looking 'systems'. And yet it may be that you still find yourself working long hours and not getting enough time for the things that are really important to you.

This book is different. It is different for two reasons. First, the core idea of the book is mind-numbingly simple and the techniques that flow from that core idea are equally simple. There are no prescriptive methods or complex flowcharts or forms to be filled out. You don't have to buy special stationery or organisers or tools. Instead you learn one simple idea, three simple techniques and you're up and running. And in case you can't wait to find out, the simple idea is that of 'not doing things' and the three simple techniques are:

- Saying 'no' nicely;
- Prioritising viciously;
- A little planning is better than a lot of firefighting.

3

The other reason the book is different is that it is not a one-size-fits-all solution. People are different. Different things work for different people. An idea or method or technique that will transform one person's life will leave somebody else cold. I have seen this over and over again in teaching this material. *Work Less, Achieve More* allows for that. It is basically a huge menu of things to try. All of the things on the menu work. All you need to do is to find the stuff on the menu that works best for you.

I have taught these ideas to thousands of people over the last twenty years. They have been used in some fairly spectacular undertakings. For example, the people who planned and executed the Special Olympics World Games – the world's biggest sporting event in 2003 – were trained in and used these ideas. That event was widely regarded as an outstanding success. So we're talking thousands of satisfied customers. Nobody has ever phoned me up and said, 'I tried them and they didn't work'. You try them; they'll work for you.

If you're not happy with the way your life is at the moment, if you want to make a major change in the amount of time you spend at work, readjust your work/life balance or reshape your entire life, this book will give you the tools to do exactly that. It will also – almost certainly – significantly reduce the amount of stress you have in your life.

As I've said, the tools are not complicated – they're very simple and use very simple ideas. But if they're so simple how come everybody's not using them? The answer to that question is that to do any of the three things above requires you to change your behaviour. You have to change your habits. And unfortunately there's probably nothing harder in the world. This book can supply the ideas and the tools but you have to provide the pixie dust – the will to want to change things a little or a lot. You do that and you're in business.

The book is divided into five parts. Part One 'Essentials' describes the basic philosophy and key concepts of *Work Less, Achieve More*. It also gives you some tools to get you started. Perhaps the single most important concept in Part One is the idea of supply and demand, an idea taken from economics. I show how it also applies to time – *your* time.

You should read Part Two 'Your Job' if you want to spend a lot less time at work or fix your work/life balance. If you do the things I ask you to do in each of these chapters then by the time you complete Part Two, you should have made the changes you want to make to your working life and to your work/life balance.

Part Three 'Your Organisation' does something which I believe is unique in books of this type. People often blame the organisation for which they work for a lack of work/life balance. They blame the culture of the organisation or its management or the sector in which the organisation operates. Part Three shows you that while there may be truth in all of these things, there is usually a more fundamental issue in operation. That issue, once again, is supply and demand – this time viewed at an organisational level. Part Three talks about this issue and what can be done about it. If you are a worker in such an organisation it should explain a lot. If you are a manager in such an organisation you will see how this could all potentially be fixed or certainly improved – and your business performance improved at the same time.

Part Four is entitled 'Your Life' and shows you how to extend these ideas to your whole life. If you really want to make real, substantial, lasting change in your life, then this part of the book will enable you to do that.

Finally, both as a way of inspiring and encouraging you and to give you further ideas on how you could use the tools, Part Five is devoted to case studies. These are people who weren't happy with their work/life balance and decided to do something about it. They used the techniques described in this book and their experiences and achievements are described in Part Five. You can use these to find somebody whose situation is perhaps similar to your own and use their experiences as a guide to help you.

These ideas work. All that's required from you is to give them a shot. The actor Michael Caine is only one of the people whom I've heard say that 'life is not a rehearsal'. Indeed it's not. Life is a performance. In fact, for each of us it's *the* performance – the only one we're going to get to give. Make sure you make yours a good one.

PART ONE: ESSENTIALS

The first part of the book gives you:
- The essential ideas behind working less and achieving more (Chapter 1);
- Some insights into your own situation (Chapters 2 and 3);
- Some quick wins (Chapter 2).

Chapter 2 also contains the first 30-day calendar for you to follow.

CHAPTER 1

The Basic Idea

Time management and extreme time management

During any given day/week/month/year or indeed, your whole life, there are always a bunch of things contending for your time and attention.

These things come from a variety of sources:
- Things you have to do – your job, the weekly shopping, paying your bills and so on;
- Things you like to do – your hobbies, spending time with your family or friends, travel etc;
- Things you hate to do but have to do anyway – paying your taxes, waiting in queues or traffic jams, that kind of thing;
- Things you would really like to do if you got the chance – that ambition you've always secretly (or not so secretly) nursed.

Each of these things wants to be done, wants you to spend your time and effort on it. Think of each of these things as a building block. Now think of the overall pile as a great tower of building blocks tottering its way up to the heavens.

During the corresponding day/week/month/year/life, there is another pile of things. This is the pile of things that you will actually do that day/week/month/year/life. For most people the second pile is many times lower than the first pile. In other words you can't do everything. Some things get done but many things remain undone.

If you go on a conventional time management course or read a time management book or invest in a time management 'system' then – unless it's a very bad course/book/system – you should be able to improve the amount of stuff you can get through every day.

But time management doesn't in any way solve the more fundamental problem. How do I make everything in the first pile fit into the second pile? How do I get all this stuff done? How do I marry the demands of my job with those of my family and of the society within which I live and my desire to put time into my hobbies/interests and my personal aspirations for my life? How can I get through this enormous pile of stuff given that there are only twenty-four hours in a day, 365 days in a year and an unknown (but finite!) number of years in my life?

There's only one answer. It's simple, it's obvious and – for many people – it's utterly terrifying.

The only answer to this question, the only logical solution to this problem is that *you're going to have to find ways to not do a vast amount of things*. This is the only way you can ensure that the right things get done – and by 'right' I mean the things that are important to you.

Conventional time management plays around the fringes of this problem. It enables you to get a bit more stuff done thereby giving the illusion that you have solved the problem described above. But you haven't solved the problem, and conventional time management won't solve it. For that you need something far more radical. If you want to solve this problem you need **extreme time management**. Extreme time management is the idea that *we're not going to do lots of things*.

This, then, is going to be our overall philosophy. And notice that this is not something that is commonly taught. Indeed, quite the opposite. From an early age we are programmed to *do* things. We start our school life as a child with our teacher giving us things to do which we have to accept. Then, as our school career progresses we get homework, projects, assignments. If we go on to some kind of third-level education we get theses, dissertations, term papers, projects. Finally, we arrive in a job and from then on until we retire, it's going to be objectives, key results areas, job descriptions – always things we have to do.

But you actually have to be able to *not do* huge quantities of stuff. Yes, I'm talking to you! You have to develop skills that will enable you to do this. Not doing stuff is as essential a business skill as any other skill you have learned in your career – chairing a meeting, writing a report or anything else.

Extreme time management. Working less but achieving more. If you're not up for it, then maybe you should read the next section.

On wake-up calls

In the first case study in Chapter 16, the writer talks of 'the wake-up call' and maybe this is something a book like this can do. It can provide a wake-up call. It can open up the vista of other possibilities. But you also may be able to recognise a wake-up call for yourself.

To put it very bluntly, if you find yourself doing what I might call 'something mad' in order to keep your current life together, then you should probably consider that as a wake-up call. What is something mad?

The following would all qualify and are only some examples:

- Checking into a hospital accident and emergency department or going to the doctor because you've had a panic attack or palpitations;
- Driving dangerously or very dangerously to make some appointment or meeting or commitment;
- Dangerous – to yourself or other people – behaviour generally. Driving with a few too many drinks after work, for example – the drinks taken because of the need to 'unwind';
- Really losing control, with a family member or work colleague, over something that – by any objective standard – would not merit it. I'm talking about a situation where the response is out of all proportion to the original issue;
- Engaging in behaviour that would have to be regarded as 'weird' if anybody were to see you doing it;
- Feeling that you are 'on the edge' and one more thing will tip you over;
- Feeling that some (or all) aspect(s) of the life you are living is/are intolerable by any objective standard.

You get the idea. Life isn't meant to be like this. Sure, life will have its ups and downs but all of your life isn't meant to be like this. Life is meant to be joyous and happy and fun and an adventure and full of possibilities.

So, if it isn't for you, *it's time to do something about it*.

The funnel

Picture yourself at your desk, beavering away. Now imagine that you and your desk are actually inside a giant silo. You sit at the bottom and the top of the silo is open to the sky. People – bosses, peers, work colleagues, loved ones, family members, various officials or employees of government bodies or institutions, you yourself, anybody really – can throw stuff in the top. All of this stuff then falls down onto you where you have to deal with it. You're probably not so much sitting at your desk as slumped over it, the weight of all these requests on your shoulders and your back.

It seems to me that for many people this is daily reality. They are trapped inside a world where they have to continuously deal with an endless (and probably increasing) stream of stuff dropping onto them.

Now imagine a different picture. This time it's not a silo; it's a funnel. The same people throw the same volume of stuff in the top, but now the stuff flows down a funnel. The funnel has three filters in it and these filters screen stuff out so that only certain things get through. This model of the funnel is how we will implement extreme time management. It is how we will not do lots of things. It is how we will work less and achieve more.

Our funnel will contain three filters, as we've already said. The three filters are:
- Saying 'no' nicely;
- Prioritising viciously;
- A little planning is better than a lot of firefighting.

You can think of the three funnels like this:
- We're not going to do some stuff at all (saying 'no' nicely);
- In fact, we're only going to do the things which align with our priorities (prioritising viciously);
- And anything we *do* do, we're going to make sure we do it with the least amount of effort (a little planning is better than a lot of firefighting).

The three filters are described in Part Two of the book. Before we go there let's do some preparatory work. It begins in the next chapter where I help you to build your 'list'.

CHAPTER 2

Your List

Keeping a list

You need to know and keep track of the stuff that comes at you – the stuff that comes in at the top of the funnel. That's where keeping a list comes in. You need to keep a list of what needs to be done. Ordinary time management methods/approaches/systems spend a lot of time fretting about the list. Most time management companies, for example, offer a variety of printed forms to keep your list on. Usually these forms come packaged in an important-looking binder that you can carry around with you – in airports, to meetings, in bars to impress people. Some individuals have made a lot of money out of selling these forms and binders – so-called 'systems'. Well done to them. I wish I had thought of it.

The truth, of course, is much simpler. All you need is a piece of paper. Mine is written on the back of a page pulled from a page-a-day diary for 14 February 2008. This is what it said last Monday:

MY LIST

1. Get fit.
2. Make a living:
   (a) Writing – *The Tour;*
   (b) Project management training and consulting:
       (i) existing customers;
       (ii) new business.
3. Increase company revenue by 50%.
4. Learn a musical instrument.

Before we go any further I should say at this point that from time to time I'll be giving you examples like this from my own experience and way of working. I do this not because you need to know lots about me, but for two other reasons.

First, I want to show you how one ordinary person has applied these ideas and made them work. (You'll see further examples of other people in the case studies.) I don't know if you'd agree but I think it's better to have real-life examples rather than made-up ones. Also, I reckon I'm pretty good at this work less, achieve more business. I seem to get lots done. I can tell you that I don't work long hours and I have a great work/life balance. I've achieved this state with the ideas and techniques in this book.

A few things about the list above:
- There is a priority implied in the list. The closer something is to the top, the more important it is. I'll have lots more to say about priorities in Part Two.
- My list is not all written down. Some of it is in my head. For example, I haven't written down, 'Love my wife and children', and this is actually my first priority. Some people like to have it all written down but for me, that would be a bit too pernickety. Whatever works for you.

Making your list

Let's see how you might put together your list.

First, does it need to be written down or not? I think the answer has to be yes. If some of mine isn't it's because I've become so used to this way of thinking and working, that I don't need it all to be written down. But if you're trying to do all of this for the first time, or are trying to put some kind of structure in place, then there's really no substitute for writing it down.

Next, does it need to be written down in some kind of electronic device (organiser, computer, phone, etc.) or some kind of fancy time management binder or system? It may have sounded earlier like I was rubbishing such aids – I wasn't. They have their place and work magnificently for some people. But that's just the point. Different things work for different people.

So, in terms of writing your list, you should choose the tool or tools that will work best for you. Paper, electronic, fancy, simple, some combination of tools – again, whatever works for you.

The next thing about your list that you need to be aware of is that goals – which is what many of the things on your list are – need to be SMART. SMART is an acronym that stands for:

> **Specific**
> **Measurable**
> **Achievable**
> **Realistic**
> **Time-bound**

Here's what these things mean.

SMART

Specific: *The goal is precise, not vague. ('Climb Mount Everest' is precise; 'become a mountain climber' is vague.)*

Measurable: *It can be measured whether the goal has been achieved or not. (The goal, 'exercise more' cannot really be measured; the goal 'run a marathon in under three hours' can.)*

Achievable: *The goal is attainable as opposed to some pie-in-the-sky nonsense. (If you have never done any kind of long-distance running, then the goal 'run a marathon in under three hours next week' is probably not achievable; but 'run a mile next week' probably would be.)*

Realistic: *The goal actually makes sense. (The goal 'become as good a guitar player as John Williams in one year' makes no sense; 'learn to play the guitar in one year' does.)*

Time-bound: *The goal has a timeframe – essentially a deadline. (The goal, 'increase revenues' is not time-bound; the goal 'increase revenues in the current financial year' is.)*

As an example of this let me show you how all my goals – if I write them out fully – satisfy these criteria and are SMART.

1. Get fit. I used to run marathons. My son and I have talked about running the London Marathon together. It probably won't happen. Both of us are too busy and whatever about him, I'm not sure I want to subject my body to that kind of punishment again. What I actually want to be able to do here is get to the point where I can run five miles four times a week. This is SMART.
2. Make a living/Writing/*The Tour*. The goal here is to get a first draft of a 100,000-word novel written in six months.
3. Project management training and consulting –existing customers. The goal here is for me to deliver 100 days' training or consulting this year.
4. Project management training and consulting – new business. The goal here is for me to achieve sales of €25,000 per month for the twelve months of this year.
5. Increase company revenue by 50% (in this financial year).
6. Learn a musical instrument. Now I'll have to admit that when I started writing this book, this particular goal wasn't SMART. For example, I hadn't even decided which instrument I'd like to play. Now I've made this goal SMART because what it now is, is to make the decision about which instrument by the end of the year and to have bought that instrument. SMART! (At last!) (It's perhaps worth noting, too, how little progress I made on this goal as long as it wasn't SMART. Now I have something clear to aim towards. Only one of the benefits of SMART goals.)

To write your list you need to start by flushing out *everything* and getting it down on paper. You can use the following as prompts or as a checklist to enable you to capture everything.

1. Start with yourself. Write down all the things that are important to you personally at the moment. Things you have to do; hate to do but have to do anyway; love to do and would like to do more of; really want to do. What hobbies or interests do you have or what things do you like to do? What are the things you've always wanted to do but have never got around to? Are there specific things you want to get done this year?
2. Now extend it out a bit. What about your home life, your immediate

family and then your wider family? Write down whatever comes to mind.

3. Next, what about your job? What's the list for that? Add these items to your list.

4. Have a quick scan through the case studies in Part Five of the book if you're looking for further prompts. If anything else occurs to you add it to your list.

5. This is your first-cut list.

Go do it!

Write down your first-cut list.

Your list is dynamic

Your list is not fixed. It's dynamic. It changes. Mine changed when I signed the contract to write this book, for instance. I had been working on a novel whose working title is *The Tour*. Now I'm going to have to put that on ice while I get this book written. So this is how my list now looks:

MY LIST

1. **Get fit.**
2. **Make a living:**
   (a) Writing
       [(i) *The Tour*;]
       (ii) *Work Less, Achieve More*
   (b) Project management training and consulting:
       (i) existing customers;
       (ii) new business.
3. **Increase company revenue by 50%.**
4. **Learn a musical instrument.**

The square brackets round *The Tour* mean that this is out of the priority list for the moment, i.e. it has no priority, i.e. it is not going to get worked on again until this book is done. So – the list can change. (And in case you're wondering, the new item on my list – to write this book – is SMART. I must deliver 60,000 words which are acceptable to the publisher by 30 September.)

You also need a diary

You also need to have some way of tracking appointments. You can use a paper diary; Outlook; the latest and hottest electronic organising device, your mobile phone; the binder they gave you at the time management course or a free one you got at Christmas from the milkman that fits into your top pocket.

I used to use a *Far Side* diary that my daughter would give me every Christmas. Because a few different people need to be aware of my diary, I switched to an electronic form so that I could email it around. I keep it in Excel.

With your list that you developed earlier and a diary to keep track of appointments, you have everything you need by way of infrastructure to work less and achieve more.

Your daily list

Most time management approaches talk about some variant on yearly, six-monthly, monthly, weekly, daily objectives/lists. That's a bit too complicated and clunky for my liking.

It seems to me that where you'll win or lose the battle will be at the daily level. The things you choose to do or not do every day will determine how much progress you make towards the things on your life list. So you need to have a daily list. You need to decide every day what things will and won't be done. Here's what a daily list might look like. This is mine for one of the days when I was writing this book.

MY DAILY LIST

To be written:
- 1,000 words of book – A
- Email inbox – A

To do:
- Exercising – A
- Teach last day of 3-day course – A
- Meet Hugh – A

Phone calls:
- Cecile – A
- Clare – A

In addition here's something that one of the case study people spoke about and that may resonate with you. She said, 'When I make my own lists daily I very rarely get through everything on them which leaves me feeling frustrated. I feel a bit anxious looking at the list today because I think mentally I had told myself I should have got up to number seven [on the list] and I only got up to number four.'

This feeling of frustration and anxiety that we're not getting through everything we intended to get through can be very dislocating. We're working on one thing but our mind is elsewhere, fretting on all the other things that aren't being done. Eventually, we can't take it any more and we hop to some other thing. But then we start to fret about the first thing. And there are always all these other things which we haven't even begun to tackle. Not only that, our mind is always elsewhere so we don't give anything the attention it really deserves.

The following approach eliminates all of these issues because we *decide* at the beginning of the day what is and what isn't going to be done.

Here's how:

1. Look at your life list and see what things require some action by you today. For any that do, write what needs to be done on your daily list.
2. Look at your diary and see if there's anything else – appointments and suchlike – that need to go on to the daily list.
3. Ask yourself is there any other thing from any other source that might possibly need to be done today.
4. This list is your list of contenders – your list of things that could be done.
5. Now mark each item on the list with one of the letters A, B, C, D.

6. Here's what the letters mean:

   A: I have to get this done today. Planets will collide, stars will fall, bosses will be grumpy, share prices will nosedive if this thing isn't done. Be as vicious as you can about the As. Is it really that important? Why can't it wait? See also further comments below.

   B: It'd be nice to get it done today.

   C: Realistically I'm not going to get this done today.

   D: Delegate it. I can get somebody else to do this.

7. Do all the Ds first i.e. get these items delegated.

8. Now do all the As.

9. When you've finished all the As, stop. Go home. Go on – go! Away with you! Off you go! What about the Bs and Cs? The answer is forget about them – they're for another day.

A couple of points. What happens if something new comes in during the day? Well then, what you do is insert this item onto your list and give it a classification. You do it if it's an A or a D and leave it otherwise.

What happens if the end of the day comes and one of your As isn't done? Well then, it can't have been an A, can it? Notice when this happens and use this knowledge to make your classification of As more vicious and strict and brutal. You should soon get really good at it.

I like to organise my list into (a) stuff to be written, (b) phone calls to be made and (c) meetings or other stuff to be done e.g. exercising. Here's my daily list from above again.

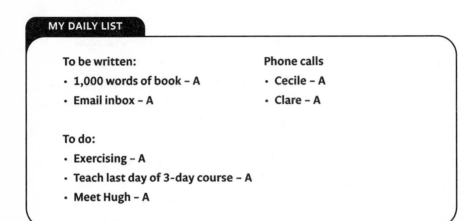

MY DAILY LIST

To be written:
- **1,000 words of book – A**
- **Email inbox – A**

Phone calls
- **Cecile – A**
- **Clare – A**

To do:
- **Exercising – A**
- **Teach last day of 3-day course – A**
- **Meet Hugh – A**

I usually write my daily list absolutely first thing in the morning or – and this is much better – last thing the previous night. If I do it in the morning it's always – and I mean always – the first thing I do. Doing it the previous night is much better though. Make it the last thing you do before you go home. This is better because the items on your list slip into your subconscious, bubble away and often – in the morning – you have greater clarity or insight into them. If you've ever woken up with the solution to a problem that you couldn't find the previous day, then you'll know what I mean.

GO DO IT

1. Make your daily list for today.
2. Rate the jobs A through D as we just described.
3. Do the As and Ds as we just described.
4. Make your daily list for tomorrow and rate it.
5. Tick off or highlight Day 1 on the 30-day calendar at the end of this chapter.
6. Go home.

Holding the gains

As we've said already, this whole business is all about replacing old behaviours with new ones, old habits with new ones. If you have done the exercise above then you have tried out the new habit. But, in general, that's not going to be enough to make it stick. You need to do it every day until you can't remember a time when you did things any other way. People who know about behaviour change reckon that it takes at least 21 days to change a habit through repetition. Hence the 30-day calendar at the end of this chapter. Photocopy it if you don't want to mess up your book and do what the 30-day calendar says for the next 30 days.

Dealing with the unexpected

It may be that you're finding that this A and D business works fine some

days, but other days your good intentions are blown away by events –
interruptions, crises, firefighting, that kind of thing. Here's how to deal
with that.

For the next five days – we're just looking at working days now – keep a
record of how much of your time gets soaked up each day in interruptions
and firefighting. Let's say, for instance, it came out like this:

MY DAILY LIST

Day	M	T	W	T	F	TOTAL	AVG.
Time spent on unplanned stuff (in hours)	2	3	1.5	6	2.5	15	3

This means that, on average, 3 (15 hours divided by 5 days) hours per day
of your time is spent on unexpected stuff. Fair enough. Next week then,
factor that into your daily list. Do this by putting an A item on your list
called 'Time for the unexpected – 3 hours'. Notice then that if you had a
week like the following:

MY DAILY LIST

Day	M	T	W	T	F	TOTAL	AVG.
Time spent on unplanned stuff (in hours)	4	3	3	2	0.5	12.5	2.5

It would only be on the Monday that the unexpected stuff would cause you
to have to stay late. Every other day you'd be sorted!

GO DO IT

1. If unexpected stuff is an issue for you then record how much of your time goes into unexpected stuff over days 8 through 12 (the weekdays of the second week).

2. At the end of the week calculate how many hours per day, on average, were spent on unexpected stuff. Do this by dividing the total number of hours spent on unexpected stuff that week by 5.

GO DO IT

If unexpected stuff is an issue for you, then – for the third week (days 15 through 19) – allow an A task every day to cover unexpected stuff. Use the average you calculated in the previous exercise as the time you'll allow for this task.

What about the 'little things'?

During the early part of our work together, one of the case study volunteers said this: 'My usual approach is to write a big list then split it up into what needs to be done each day, but I would usually do the things that I think will be quite quick first, but then they always take longer than you think, so I don't get round to the big things.' And also, 'However, I did find that about five or six other things came up during the day that I needed to respond to that day, I found it easier to do them straight away than wait, but with hindsight should I have just added them to the list and carried on with my main task first?'

She describes situations that many of us encounter. We all have 'other things', 'little things', 'quick things', 'small stuff', 'the things that I think will be quite quick'. We decide to clear the decks of these so that we can then devote time to the things that really matter. In doing this I think we make a fundamental mistake – and unfortunately, it's a mistake that many conventional time management books and systems actively encourage. In doing so I think they highlight again the difference between time management and extreme time management.

For example, there is a hugely successful time management book out at the moment called *Getting Things Done* by David Allen. In it, the author talks about the 'two-minute rule'. The two-minute rule says that if you can get something done in less than two minutes then you should do so. Clear the decks. Get it out of the way. This is fine and dandy if you just aim to be a sort of productivity machine i.e. to increase your efficiency, your throughput.

But if you're trying to work less and achieve more i.e. if you're trying not to do things, then the two-minute rule won't work. You'll get lots of small stuff done and that will steal time – precious, irreplaceable time – from the important things. So forget about the two-minute rule. Here's how to deal with the situation described above.

1. If you have a bunch of small things to do, the first thing to ask yourself is, which ones – if any – *really* need to be done today? It's the old A, B, C, D thing again. So rate them.

2. Now if you also know – as in the case study above – that it's inevitable that other things will pop up during the day *that will have to be done* i.e. will be As, then set a time in your day when you're going to get all the As done. This means that there will be a planned time when you will do both the As you currently know about plus the other inevitable As that will pop up during the day. But notice that not everything that pops up during the day will be an A – and if it's not then don't do it. And you can use the technique we discussed in the previous section to figure out how much time you'll need for the surprise As.

Working ahead

Finally, here's a really neat idea. If you get all of today's As done, rather than going home you could start doing tomorrow's work. In other words, make tomorrow's list, classify the items A through D, delegate the Ds and start on the As. Now you're doing tomorrow's work today! This is 'working ahead'. By doing it you should find that you have fewer things to do towards the end of the week. The result of that could be a stress-free Friday or going home early or – if you have some form of flexitime – maybe a Friday off and a long weekend!

GO DO IT

'Work ahead' for the rest of the month – see the 30-day calendar for detailed instructions.

30-DAY CALENDAR

1	2	3	4
1 Make and rate your list. 2 Do the As and Ds. 3 Make your list for tomorrow. 4 Go home.	1 Make and rate your list. 2 Do the As and Ds. 3 Make your list for tomorrow. 4 Go home.	1 Make and rate your list. 2 Do the As and Ds. 3 Make your list for tomorrow. 4 Go home.	1 Make and rate your list. 2 Do the As and Ds. 3 Make your list for tomorrow. 4 Go home.

8	9	10	11
1 Make and rate your list. 2 Do the As and Ds. 3 Record how much time goes into unexpected stuff. 4 Make your list for tomorrow. 5 Go home.	1 Make and rate your list. 2 Do the As and Ds. 3 Record how much time goes into unexpected stuff. 4 Make your list for tomorrow. 5 Go home.	1 Make and rate your list. 2 Do the As and Ds. 3 Record how much time goes into unexpected stuff. 4 Make your list for tomorrow. 5 Go home.	1 Make and rate your list. 2 Do the As and Ds. 3 Record how much time goes into unexpected stuff. 4 Make your list for tomorrow. 5 Go home.

15	16	17	18
1 Make and rate your list, if you haven't already. 2 Allow an A for unexpected stuff. 3 Do the As and Ds. 4 Record how much time goes into unexpected stuff. 5 Make your list for tomorrow. 6 Go home.	1 Make and rate your list, if you haven't already. 2 Allow an A for unexpected stuff. 3 Do the As and Ds. 4 Record how much time goes into unexpected stuff. 5 Make your list for tomorrow. 6 Go home.	1 Make and rate your list, if you haven't already. 2 Allow an A for unexpected stuff. 3 Do the As and Ds. 4 Record how much time goes into unexpected stuff. 5 Make your list for tomorrow. 6 Go home.	1 Make and rate your list, if you haven't already. 2 Allow an A for unexpected stuff. 3 Do the As and Ds. 4 Record how much time goes into unexpected stuff. 5 Make your list for tomorrow. 6 Go home.

22	23	24	25
1 Make and rate your list, if you haven't already. 2 Allow an A for unexpected stuff. 3 Do the As and Ds. 4 Record how much time goes into unexpected stuff. 5 Make your list for tomorrow. 6 Do some or all of tomorrow's list today. 7 Be sure you finish the day with a list of stuff to be done tomorrow. 8 Go home.	1 Make and rate your list, if you haven't already. 2 Allow an A for unexpected stuff. 3 Do the As and Ds. 4 Record how much time goes into unexpected stuff. 5 Make your list for tomorrow. 6 Do some or all of tomorrow's list today. 7 Be sure you finish the day with a list of stuff to be done tomorrow. 8 Go home.	1 Make and rate your list, if you haven't already. 2 Allow an A for unexpected stuff. 3 Do the As and Ds. 4 Record how much time goes into unexpected stuff. 5 Make your list for tomorrow. 6 Do some or all of tomorrow's list today. 7 Be sure you finish the day with a list of stuff to be done tomorrow. 8 Go home.	1 Make and rate your list, if you haven't already. 2 Allow an A for unexpected stuff. 3 Do the As and Ds. 4 Record how much time goes into unexpected stuff. 5 Make your list for tomorrow. 6 Do some or all of tomorrow's list today. 7 Be sure you finish the day with a list of stuff to be done tomorrow. 8 Go home.

29

1 Make and rate your list, if you haven't already.
2 Allow an A for unexpected stuff.
3 Do the As and Ds.
4 Record how much time goes into unexpected stuff.
5 Make your list for tomorrow.
6 Do some or all of tomorrow's list today.
7 Be sure you finish the day with a list of stuff to be done tomorrow.
8 Go home.

5	6	7
1 Make and rate your list.	1 Make and rate your list.	1 Make and rate your list.
2 Do the As and Ds.	2 Do the As and Ds.	2 Do the As and Ds.
3 Make your list for tomorrow.	3 Make your list for tomorrow.	3 Make your list for tomorrow.
4 Go home.		

12	13	14
1 Make and rate your list.	1 Make and rate your list.	1 Make and rate your list.
2 Do the As and Ds.	2 Do the As and Ds.	2 Do the As and Ds.
3 Record how much time goes into unexpected stuff.	3 Record how much time goes into unexpected stuff.	3 Record how much time goes into unexpected stuff.
4 Make your list for tomorrow.	4 Make your list for tomorrow.	4 Make your list for tomorrow.
5 Go home.		

19	20	21
1 Make and rate your list, if you haven't already.	1 Make and rate your list, if you haven't already.	1 Make and rate your list, if you haven't already.
2 Allow an A for unexpected stuff.	2 Allow an A for unexpected stuff.	2 Allow an A for unexpected stuff.
3 Do the As and Ds.	3 Do the As and Ds.	3 Do the As and Ds.
4 Record how much time goes into unexpected stuff.	4 Record how much time goes into unexpected stuff.	4 Record how much time goes into unexpected stuff.
5 Make your list for tomorrow.	5 Make your list for tomorrow.	5 Make your list for tomorrow.
6 Go home.		

26	27	28
1 Make and rate your list, if you haven't already.	1 Make and rate your list, if you haven't already.	1 Make and rate your list, if you haven't already.
2 Allow an A for unexpected stuff.	2 Allow an A for unexpected stuff.	2 Allow an A for unexpected stuff.
3 Do the As and Ds.	3 Do the As and Ds.	3 Do the As and Ds.
4 Record how much time goes into unexpected stuff.	4 Record how much time goes into unexpected stuff.	4 Record how much time goes into unexpected stuff.
5 Make your list for tomorrow.	5 Make your list for tomorrow.	5 Make your list for tomorrow.
6 Do some or all of tomorrow's list today.	6 Do some or all of tomorrow's list today.	6 Do some or all of tomorrow's list today.
7 Be sure you finish the day with a list of stuff to be done tomorrow.	7 Be sure you finish the day with a list of stuff to be done tomorrow.	7 Be sure you finish the day with a list of stuff to be done tomorrow.
8 Go home.		

30

1 Make and rate your list, if you haven't already.
2 Allow an A for unexpected stuff.
3 Do the As and Ds.
4 Record how much time goes into unexpected stuff.
5 Make your list for tomorrow.
6 Do some or all of tomorrow's list today.
7 Be sure you finish the day with a list of stuff to be done tomorrow.
8 Go home.

CHAPTER 3

Supply and Demand

After Chapter 2 you should have a much clearer insight into the things that are placing demands upon your time. Now you're ready to start thinking in terms of supply and demand.

How is it that some people seem to get a whole lot more done than others? We think of people like generals or politicians or well-known businessmen. They seem to be able to get their incredibly responsible and important jobs done but still find time, for example, to exercise.

'They have armies of flunkies,' I hear you say. Sure, there may be some truth in that. They have people to whom they can delegate things. 'They're workaholics,' you offer, and again some of them are, but many aren't and have time for lives that are full and varied and balanced and fulfilling. 'They manage on a few hours' sleep.' Yes, this might be true of some of them – Margaret Thatcher is a well-known example – but that's not the full answer either.

It seems to me that at least part of the key lies in the fact that these people are very conscious that time is a quantity that can be thought of in terms of supply and demand.

The phrase 'supply and demand' was first used by James Denham-Steuart in his *Inquiry into the Principles of Political Economy*, published in 1767. The term related to the supply of goods and the demand for them. But supply and demand is a far more general concept. We can think of supply and demand in our personal finances, for instance. Demand – the cost of our lifestyle – and supply – our income. And we can think of supply and demand in terms of time. Demand is everything we have to do; supply is the time available to do it. The problem of the two piles of stuff that we discussed in Chapter 1 is the problem of supply (time available) and demand (things wanting to be done).

For nearly twenty years now, I have been getting people to measure the supply and demand of their time, and two things have become very evident to me. Most people underestimate demand (how much they have to do) and overestimate supply (how much time is available). For example, when someone is late for an appointment or a deadline, this is exactly what they have done. Or you ask a work colleague if they can give you some of their time to work on a project of yours. Almost always people agree because they are the proverbial team players and anxious to help. It has been my experience that often people end up committing time that they don't really have. If people do enough of this then they end up overloaded, stressed and failing to deliver on commitments.

If you are going to work less and achieve more then you need to start becoming more aware of your time as supply and demand quantities. How to do that is the subject of this chapter. You're not just going to become more aware of your supply and demand, timewise – you're going to measure it.

Supply and Demand Calculator

The Supply and Demand Calculator is the fancy name for something that we also call a 'Dance Card'. The name 'Dance Card' refers to those more genteel times where, when a woman went to a dance or ball, she was given a card with a list of the tunes that the band or orchestra was going to play. To request a dance with a woman a gentleman wrote his name against a particular dance, i.e. he booked that dance with that woman. The Dance Card measured supply (the number of dances available) and demand (the number of dances booked).

To calculate your Dance Card, your supply and demand, do the following.

Figure out everything you have to do – Demand

1. Pick a period of time – a month, a couple of months, from now to the end of next month, from now to the end of the quarter, half a year, the rest of the year – whatever suits you.
2. Make a list of all the projects you will be working on during the period that you've chosen. Include on the list any project which:

- Ends during the period that you've chosen;
- Starts during the period you've chosen;
- Starts and ends in the period you've chosen;
- Runs through the period that you've chosen.

3. Now add to the list what might be called 'business as usual' or 'day-job' type things. These would be things like:
   - Meetings. All your meetings may be about particular projects, but most of us have things like 'the group meeting', 'the Monday meeting', 'company meeting' and so on. Don't forget too that you may have to do preparation before a meeting, there will be the meeting itself and you may have to do follow-ups or action items afterwards.
   - Reports. Maybe your job involves producing (or reading) a lot of these.
   - Interruptions. Whether they come person-to-person or by phone (landline or mobile), every one of us has these every day.
   - Inbox/Email. Possibly all of your emails are related to specific projects, but most of us have other stuff we have to deal with every day. And anyway, there's the time involved in figuring out whether they're about specific projects or not.
   - Trips/Visits. Maybe you're going on a business-related trip or somebody's coming to visit you and that will soak up your time.
   - Training. Maybe you're involved in some form of training course or you're coaching or mentoring somebody else.
   - Annual leave/vacation/holidays.
   - Managing people. Maybe you're the line manager of a number of people and this takes up your time.
   - Phone calls/conference calls. We all have some/a lot of these to do every day.
   - Support. Maybe you support products or systems or people in some way.
   - Recruitment. Maybe your organisation is expanding and you have to spend time looking at CVs, interviewing people and doing related activities.
   - Firefighting.

- Filling in for people. Maybe you're standing in for people who are away on some kind of leave.

4. Add an additional line item called, 'New stuff'. It may be that in your job nothing is going to change over the period that you're looking at. (I've heard there are jobs like that though I've never come across one myself!) Presumably, what's more likely is that new things will come along. We don't know what they are yet because they haven't come along – we just know it's inevitable that they will. 'New stuff' is to cover these.

Figure out how much time it will take to do it

Now figure out how much of your time is going to go into each of the items on your list over the period that you're looking at. Use hours per day, days per week, total hours, total days or whatever measure seems most appropriate to each line item. Be sure to record each of the amounts of time in the same units. I find days are best for this.

Add all of these up. This gives you the total amount of work you have to do in the period in question.

Figure out how much time you have available – Supply

Now figure out how many work days there are in the same period. (Convert that number to hours if you've been using hours in the previous section.) This is how much time you have available.

We have a little Excel spreadsheet called a Supply and Demand Calculator that will enable you to do this quickly. It's shown here. If you want a copy, send me an email at the address shown in the back of the book and I'll send it back to you. There are some examples of supply demand calculations at the end of this chapter to also help you.

> **GO DO IT**
>
> Calculate your supply and demand as described above.

ETP SUPPLY AND DEMAND CALCULATOR

YOUR PROJECTS	Project names	Hours	Days
1		0	0
2		0	0
3		0	0
4		0	0
5		0	0
6		0	0
...		0	0

BUSINESS AS USUAL/'DAY JOB'		
Preparing/writing reports	0	0
Attending training	0	0
Training other people	0	0
Managing people	0	0
Annual leave	0	0
Email/Inbox	0	0
Interruptions	0	0
Phone calls	0	0
Trips	0	0
Visits	0	0
Meetings	0	0
Filling in for people	0	0
Recruitment	0	0
Public holidays	0	0
Other	0	0
New stuff	0	0
TOTAL	0	0

Number of weeks for which you want to calculate availability	4
Number of days per week that you work	5
Total number of work days in the period you've chosen	20
Number of hours per day that you work	8
Total number of hours available in the period that you're looking at	160

EXPLANATION

STEP	CELL(S)	DESCRIPTION	ACTION
1	L4	The number of weeks for which you want to calculate availability	Accept the default of 4 weeks or enter to override
2	L5	The number of days per week that you work	Accept the default of 5 days per week or enter to override
3	L6	Total number of work days in the period that you've chosen	Calculated (L4 multiplied by L5)
4	L7	The number of hours per day you work	Accept the default of 8 hours per day or enter to override
5	L8	The number of hours per week you work	Calculated (L6 multiplied by L7)
6*	B4-B10	The names of your projects. Include any project which starts, ends, starts and ends, or passes through the period you've chosen	Enter the names of your projects
7*	B13-B26	Business as usual/'day job' things	Select which of these apply to you
8	B28	This is to cover new things that come along in the next 4 weeks. (In most jobs it's inevitable that new things will come along.	No action

CONTINUED

STEP	CELL(S)	DESCRIPTION	ACTION
9	Columns C & D	Column C is your time measured in hours; D is your time measured in days	Choose either hours (Col C) or days (Col D) as the units for recording your time. If you choose hours, then carry out Steps 10-12. If you choose days then carry out Steps 13-15
10	C4–C10	The amount of your time (in hours) that will go into each of these over the next 4 weeks	Estimate it in total hours or hours per day (and then multiply it by the total number of days (L6))
11	C13–C26	The amount of your time (in hours) that will go into each of these over the next 4 weeks	Estimate it in total hours or hours per day (and then multiply it by the total number of days (L6))
12	C28	The amount of your time (in hours) that will be soaked up by new things over the next 4 weeks	Estimate/guess it, i.e. pick a number
13	D4–D10	The amount of your time (in days) that will go into each of these over the next 4 weeks	Estimate it in total days or days per week (and multiply by 4)
14	D13–D26	The amount of your time (in days) that will go into each of these over the next 4 weeks	Estimate it in total days or days per week (and multiply by 4)
15	D28	The amount of your time (in days) that will be soaked up by new things over the next 4 weeks	Estimate/guess it, i.e. pick a number
16	C30	Total work you have to do in the next 4 weeks (in hours)	Calculated
17	D30	Total work you have to do in the next 4 weeks (in days)	Calculated
		*Add more rows if necessary	Now you can compare C30 with L8 or D30 with L6 to see how much time is available

Supply and demand – the brutal facts

I don't know whether you were surprised by your supply and demand calculation or not – most people are. But whether you are or not, I hope that two things are abundantly clear:

• You're only going to be able to do some things – and the corollary of this is that you're not going to be able to do many other things.
• The things that you do decide to do had better be bloody important.

If you regard hugging your children or learning to play the piano or climbing Mount Everest or whatever, as important, then you're going to have to find the time for them. And that will mean taking time away from other things.

How you're going to do these two things:
- Not devote time to the things that don't matter
- Devote time to the things that do

is another way of thinking about extreme time management.

Examples

Here are a couple of examples of supply and demand calculations just to help you in drawing up your own. Figure 3.1 contains one for a six-month period. (The calculations assume 20 days in a month and four days in a week.)

FIGURE 3.1

		120	20	20	20	20	20	20
Job	Needs	Jan	Feb	Mar	Apr	May	Jun
Project X	72 days	12	12	12	12	12	12
Project Y	24 days	8	8	4	4		
Project Z	10 days				2	4	4
Selling	2 dpw	8	8	8	8	8	8
Email/ Inbox/ Admin	1.25 dpw	5	5	5	5	5	5
Holidays	10 days						10
Total work to do	194	33	33	29	31	29	39

The column headed 'Job' lists all of the things that this person is involved in – their 'list'. The next column indicates how much work is estimated to go into these things over the period under investigation. Days per month (dpm), days per week (dpw), hours per day or just plain days are all good ways of calculating how much work needs to be done. Then the remaining columns show how this time will be spread out over the period under investigation – in this case, six months.

There are two other items of interest. The top row of figures in italics shows how many days are available per month. The total of these is 120. (Note that rather than trying to allow for the different numbers of working days in different countries, I have assumed that every month consists of 20 days. You could adjust this up or down for your own situation. For example, in Europe, December is definitely not 20 working days in most companies.) The other item of interest is the total of all the work this person has to do – in this example, 194 days. In the example then, the person has an overload of more than 50 per cent, i.e. over 50 per cent more work to do than time available to do it.

The supply and demand calculation in Figure 3.1 was for a person who does a variety of projects – which take reasonably predictable amounts of time – and other kinds of work. However, supply and demand calculations can be done by anybody – even if your work is very unpredictable. If your job is like that, then the best thing to do is to record what actually happens say, in a particular week or over several weeks, and use this as your start point.

Figure 3.2 shows a supply demand calculation for such a job, with actual time spent in a given week. This one was put together using Excel, but you can do these calculations any way you like. A piece of paper – as shown in Figure 3.1 – is absolutely fine.

FIGURE 3.2

		Total hours	8 Mon	8 Tue	8 Wed	8 Thu	8 Fri	0 Sat	0 Sun	40
1	Phone calls	9.25	2.25	2.50	3.00	1.00	0.50	0.00	0.00	
2	Admin	7.50	1.75	0.50	0.75	1.50	3.00	0.00	0.00	
3	Status report to boss	1.00					1.00			
4	Running office	4.75	1.00	0.50	1.00	1.00	1.25	0.00	0.00	
5	Overseeing staff	6.25	2.00	1.00	1.00	1.25	1.00	0.00	0.00	
6	E-mail; timesheets; petty cash; stock; phone	5.25	1.00	1.25	0.75	0.75	1.50	0.00	0.00	
7	Interruptions	7.50	1.00	0.50	2.50	2.00	1.50	0.00	0.00	
8	Meetings	6.25		0.75	1.50	3.00	1.00	0.00	0.00	
9	Bringing work home	6.00		3.00				0.00	3.00	
		53.75	9.00	10.00	10.50	10.50	10.75	0.00	3.00	

Overload: 34%

PART TWO: YOUR JOB

The second part of the book describes the three powerful ideas and associated tools that will enable you to work less and achieve more. They are:
- Saying 'no' nicely (Chapter 4);
- Prioritising viciously (Chapter 5);
- A little planning is better than a lot of firefighting (Chapters 6–10).

CHAPTER 4

Saying 'No' Nicely

I've said already, numerous times, that we were going to have to learn ways of not doing stuff. The simplest way is the one we study in this chapter. If, like most of us, you have been programmed from childhood into doing lots of things, then it's time to begin reprogramming. You're going to have to learn how to wiggle out of things. You need to learn to say 'no' in such a way that you:

- Reduce the time taken to do something. Doing all your emails at once rather than responding every time your computer goes 'bing' or doing all your phone calls at once, are examples of this. Or –
- Kick the thing on to somebody else. It's called delegation. Or –
- Delay or dodge the thing for as long as possible. It's called procrastination and can be a good thing. Or –
- Don't do it at all. The best idea of all.

You need to say 'no' nicely – in a way that nobody takes offence.

GO DO IT

1. Sit down with a colleague or colleagues. Brainstorm for ten minutes and come up with as many ways as you can think of saying 'no' nicely.

2. Now try some of these out during the day.

Here are some of mine – in no particular order.

1. 'For personal reasons I won't be able to do that any more', or – almost identical, but the choice of words is often important – 'Things have changed for me and I won't be able to do that any more'.

2. Print off a sign in a large font saying *Your Lack of Planning is not My Emergency*. Hang it on your office or cubicle. While it may be on the limit of 'nicely' I think it still qualifies. I have actually seen somebody walking towards somebody's cubicle and then veering away as they read this sign.

3. As somebody comes to interrupt you, pick up the nearest piece of paper. Now put your hand to your temple and try to look like you're grappling with Einstein's Theory of General Relativity. Say, 'I'm really involved in this at the moment. Any chance you could come back in an hour?' Everybody respects it; nobody takes offence. Often they don't come back at all – great! If they do, they often have several things that they want to cover and these can now all be done together. All of us know serial interrupters!

4. Implement red time and green time. Divide your day up into periods of red time and green time. In green time you take interruptions (face-to-face, email and phone); in red time you don't. For example, you might divide a 9–5 day into 10–11 and 3–4 red time, everything else green time.

5. Pretend you have the hottest date of your life at 7 p.m. this evening. (If you're lucky maybe you do!) How would you organise your day accordingly? Well, probably something like this. You would plan to leave at 5 p.m. at the latest. You would probably say that you need to be out by 4 p.m. just to be on the safe side. The hour between 4 and 5 p.m. would be your contingency in case some genius came along to you and said, 'I need this now'. If any interruptions occurred during the day you would give them short shrift, as you would know how short and precious your time was (i.e. you would be very conscious of your supply and demand). Notice that things like having to catch a train or a plane or pick up children after work have exactly the same effect. (The date is probably more fun, though!)

6. Work from a place where people don't expect you to be – a meeting room or somebody else's desk. Work from home.

7. Get into the mindset of 'How can I *avoid* doing this?' as opposed to 'How can I do this?' This is not a bad thing. We'll be talking in Chapter 5 about knowing your priorities. Provided you know these you will want to put time into them. For everything else you should be wondering how you can avoid doing them.

8. Say, 'Fill out the form,' or, 'Could you send me an email about that?'. With luck it'll be too much trouble and they'll drop it.
9. Work a 40-hour week – see section below.
10. Decline meetings – ask why you have to be there. Ask what you're expected to contribute. Ask what you're going to gain from the meeting. Ask if you can do your bit first (and then leave).
11. Say, 'If you'll do this first then I'll do that'.
12. Say, 'I can't do that for personal reasons'. (People almost always back off and never ask.)

The 40-hour week

From biblical times to before the Industrial Revolution workers worked Monday to Saturday with Sunday (the Sabbath) off. They rose with the sun, usually toiled in the fields and went to bed when the sun set. Then came the Industrial Revolution and factories and mines became the new places of work. Soon labour unions began to organise to stop workers from being exploited. As industry spread in Western Europe and the United States, unions pushed management to reduce working hours and increase pay. The unions started by whittling away at Saturday. Eventually working hours dropped from 48 hours per week to 44 and finally to 40. In 1938 the United States Department of Labor established the 40-hour week as the standard under the Fair Labor Standards Act.

Sometimes politicians do great things and this surely, is such a time. The zen-like perfection of eight hours a day spent working, eight hours a day sleeping and eight hours a day having a good time is truly a wonderful thing. (If you're lucky – or you follow the advice in this book – then the eight hours a day spent working should become another eight hours of having a good time! The old saying 'find something you love to do and you'll never work a day in your life' is so true.)

If you've drifted from the eight-hour day you need to get back to it. I'm not saying you have to work a 40-hour week every week. I'm not saying that because it says you should work 37.25 (or whatever) hours in your contract then, damn it, that's what you're going to work. I accept that you may love your job so much that you want to work more. (Last week, for example, I worked 80 hours – a combination of a busy week of revenue-earning coupled with wanting to give this book a kick-start. However, it should be said that (a) it's probably more than ten years since I've done this, and (b) I was on the road and away from home so these hours weren't being stolen from my loved ones.)

But working long hours should be the exception rather than the rule. I have no problem with a push to make a deadline or because something genuinely unexpected has come along. But I do have a huge problem – and so should you – with sustained working of very long hours. The wife of one of the case study volunteers told me '[he] usually works an average of 65 hours a week Monday to Friday, and, in addition, is always available... via phone till midnight and at weekends'. Terrible stuff.

Working continuous long hours just makes you inefficient. To put this more simply, you achieve less than if you had only worked a 40-hour week. This is because you become careless with your time. Because you feel you have almost unlimited supply – because you're going to work all the hours God sends – you give in to almost every request, i.e. you satisfy every demand. If you're going to work less and achieve more, then you need to stop this kind of behaviour immediately.

There is a book by Tom DeMarco called *The Deadline*; it's a novel about project management. While it's hardly *War and Peace* or Pulitzer Prize-winning material, it does have some interesting things to say about people working long hours. Here's what it says in a section entitled 'The Effects of Pressure':

- People under pressure don't think any faster.
- Extended overtime is a productivity-reduction tactic.
- Short bursts of pressure and even overtime may be a useful tactic as they focus people and increase the sense that the work is important, but extended pressure is always a mistake.
- Perhaps managers make so much use of pressure because they don't know what else to do, or are daunted by how difficult the alternatives are.
- Terrible suspicion: the real reason for use of pressure and overtime may be to make everyone look better when the project fails.

So if you've drifted from the 40-hour week, you need to return to it. It is a truly wonderful way of saying 'no' nicely.

The four-day week/the nine-day fortnight

And who says you have to work all of your 40 hours – or whatever your working week is – across five days? Personally I like to work a five-day week, if only because of the great pleasure that Friday night brings. (Also I'm mostly OK about Mondays so they don't cause me too much grief.) But here are another couple of possibilities you could consider.

You could work a four-day week. You might take a bit of a hit financially – though see Case Study No. 1 for how it might not be as much as you think – but the resulting freedom you could get could be more than worth it.

I knew somebody who worked five mornings from 8:30 to 12:30 at which point she *had* to go – due to children, pickups etc. She reckoned she got as much done in those twenty hours a week as her colleagues got done in their full-time, five-day-a-week jobs.

And something we started in my company, ETP, when we were going through a bad couple of years, was the nine-day fortnight. We didn't have enough money for salary rises, so instead we offered people a nine-day fortnight, i.e. Monday to Friday followed by Monday to Thursday. There were a few simple rules. The eight hours of the second Friday was made up by everybody extending their nine working days by 50 minutes. Each department had to make sure there was adequate coverage on Fridays e.g. both people in the Admin department couldn't be off together on Friday. Other than that there was very little to it by way of management or administration. The people loved it – every second week was a short week and every second weekend was a long weekend.

Figuring out where your time goes

Here is perhaps the easiest way in the world to get motivated to say 'no' nicely. Use a Supply and Demand Calculator as described in Chapter 3, but instead of projecting into the future as to where your time might go, use the calculator to record where your time *actually* goes. Write down all your projects plus business as usual stuff as before, but now record how much of your time goes into each of these over say, a week. However, also record when your time goes into other things that you hadn't expected or written down on the Supply and Demand Calculator originally. I'm thinking of things like interruptions, chats with people, little firefights or questions or timewasters that pop up. Do this for a week and you'll probably be amazed at how much of your time just disappears. Think then of how much extra time you would have if this time didn't disappear. Look at how much earlier you could go home each day – or how much more you could get done. I'm not saying that you shouldn't be sociable with people at work but for many people there is lots of time to be saved here.

> **GO DO IT**
>
> 1. Try out the 30-day calendar on pages 54–55.
>
> 2. If you're already doing the 30-day calendar from Chapter 2 – the one for processing your daily list – then that's no problem, you can do this one in parallel. There's nothing to stop you changing two habits at once!

Saying 'no' nicely to email

If ever something could be described as both a blessing and a curse, it is email. The capability to write a letter or memo and, with no other work, send it pretty much instantaneously to another party is an extraordinary innovation. No taking it to the post office, no printing it off and putting it on a fax machine, no waiting several days while it gets physically transported to the other place. Our ancestors would have been astonished and it's probably true to say that the course of history could have been quite different had this facility been available to kings, generals, politicians and other people who shaped the world.

But it's also a curse. One of my case studies said she spent four hours a day 'doing emails'. I am convinced that there are people in the world who have become, quite literally, slaves to email. I believe there are people who, when they die, will have as their epitaph, 'Here lies Charlie – he kept an empty inbox'.

If this is you or if email is just a big headache for you, you need to start dealing with the problem. Saying 'no' nicely is a way of doing that. In terms of practising the skill of saying 'no' nicely, it can be a very good place to start.

Email is a tool that you use – just like say, a pencil or a computer or a whiteboard. Imagine if every time you saw a pencil anywhere, you just had to pick it up and start writing with it. Or that every time you saw a computer you just had to sit down and work at it. Or every whiteboard you saw you had to grab a marker and start covering it in writing. The idea is ludicrous. We use these tools as and when we need them.

So it should be with email. There should therefore be two types of situation when you need to use it. One is when you want to communicate with other people. The other is to see if anybody has communicated with you. It seems to be the latter of these two that causes most of the problems. Either:

- We keep checking to see if anybody has communicated with us, or
- When we find they have we feel we need to reply straight away, or
- We treat all emails as equally important. There seems to be a commonly held view that an empty inbox is a good thing.

All of these behaviours are daft and the combination of the three is especially stupid. We basically say, 'I'm going to keep checking for emails and as soon as one comes in it will get answered.' Great – so you're going to become an email answering machine. Is that really what your organisation wants you to do? Is that really the extent of your ambitions? Is that really what your life is going to come down to?

If you are prone to these behaviours you need to change them pronto. We'll cure two of them here and the third one in Chapter 5. Basically you need to stop constantly responding to emails. So how will you do that? Well, for starters, if you didn't know they'd arrived, that would help, so turn off the damn thing on your computer that goes 'bing' when an email arrives. Next you need to resist the temptation to keep looking at your inbox, so how about allocating set times each day to look at them? You could do it twice a day – say first thing in the morning and just after lunch. You could allocate, say, 9:00–10:00 and 2:00–3:00.

Now I know you're perhaps panicking at this point. With the twice-a-day suggestion, worst case, something could arrive just after 10:00 and it could be 2:00 p.m. (nearly four hours later) before you saw it. Gasp! I'm not going

30-DAY CALENDAR

1	2	3	4
Using whatever techniques you have come up with say 'no' nicely for half a day, either the morning or the afternoon.	Do whatever you want.	Using whatever techniques you have come up with say 'no' nicely for half a day, either the morning or the afternoon.	Do whatever you want.
8	**9**	**10**	**11**
Do whatever you want.	Using whatever techniques you have come up with say 'no' nicely for half a day, either the morning or the afternoon.	Do whatever you want.	Using whatever techniques you have come up with say 'no' nicely for half a day, either the morning or the afternoon.
15	**16**	**17**	**18**
Say 'no' nicely for the whole day.	Do whatever you want.	Say 'no' nicely for the whole day.	Do whatever you want.
22	**23**	**24**	**25**
Start today and see what is the longest continuous period of time that you can say 'no' nicely for. Try and build it up. A week would be a good and impressive target. If you fail, reset the clock and start again.	See Day 22.	See Day 22.	See Day 22.
29	**30**		
See Day 22.	See Day 22.		

5	6	7
Using whatever techniques you have come up with say 'no' nicely for half a day, either the morning or the afternoon.	Say 'no' nicely to something over the weekend. Say no to something you *didn't* want to do and use the time saved for something you *did* want to do.	Say 'no' nicely to something over the weekend. Say no to something you *didn't* want to do and use the time saved for something you *did* want to do.

12	13	14
Say 'no' nicely for the whole day.	Say 'no' nicely to something over the weekend. Say no to something you *didn't* want to do and use the time saved for something you *did* want to do.	Say 'no' nicely to something over the weekend. Say no to something you *didn't* want to do and use the time saved for something you *did* want to do.

19	20	21
Say 'no' nicely for the whole day.	Say 'no' nicely to something over the weekend. Say no to something you *didn't* want to do and use the time saved for something you *did* want to do.	Say 'no' nicely to something over the weekend. Say no to something you *didn't* want to do and use the time saved for something you *did* want to do.

26	27	28
See Day 22.	Say 'no' nicely to something over the weekend. Say no to something you *didn't* want to do and use the time saved for something you *did* want to do.	Say 'no' nicely to something over the weekend. Say no to something you *didn't* want to do and use the time saved for something you *did* want to do.

to push you too hard at this point. I think twice a day works for most people but I accept that your job may be different. What I want to do, though, is to get you into the habit of only checking a certain number of times every day. So:

1. Decide how many times a day you're going to check your email. Once is ideal; twice is good; three times is acceptable; four times is pushing it. Anything more than four and you're kidding yourself – you're just indulging in the old behaviour.

2. Set times to do this. For example:
   Twice: 9:00–10:00; 14:00–15:00
   Three times: 9:00–10:00; 12:00–13:00; 15:00–16:00
   Four times: 9:00–10:00; 12:00–13:00; 14:00–15:00; 16:00–17:00.

3. Stick religiously to whatever times you choose. Resist the temptation to peek outside of your fixed hours.

GO DO IT

1. If email is a problem for you then do the above for the next month according to the 30-day calendar on pages 58–59.

2. If you're already doing the 30-day calendar from Chapter 2 and the one above, then – again – that's no problem. You can do this one in parallel. There's nothing to stop you changing *three* habits at once!

Afterword on saying 'no' nicely

I hope you can see that saying 'no' nicely, by itself, actually solves the problem we discussed in Chapter 1 – the problem of the pile of stuff to be done and the pile of stuff that will actually get done. If you could become *really* good at saying 'no' nicely – and nothing else – many of your problems would disappear. That's how powerful a technique it is. If you could get to the point where I am at, for example, where your immediate reaction when somebody asks you to do something, is 'how can I get out of this?' rather than 'how can I fit this in to an already overcrowded life?', then you would be well on the way to being sorted.

But we have two more powerful ideas to go. In the next chapter we talk about what I call 'prioritising viciously'.

30-DAY CALENDAR

1	2	3	4
Set your fixed times and follow them religiously.	Set your fixed times and follow them religiously.	Set your fixed times and follow them religiously.	Set your fixed times and follow them religiously.

8	9	10	11
1 If you had allowed yourself four fixed times a day, reduce it to three and follow them religiously. Otherwise follow whatever times you have decided upon religiously. 2 At the end of the day record if reducing the number of fixed times to three caused you any serious problems.	1 If you had allowed yourself four fixed times a day, reduce it to three and follow them religiously. Otherwise follow whatever times you have decided upon religiously. 2 At the end of the day record if reducing the number of fixed times to three caused you any serious problems.	1 If you had allowed yourself four fixed times a day, reduce it to three and follow them religiously. Otherwise follow whatever times you have decided upon religiously. 2 At the end of the day record if reducing the number of fixed times to three caused you any serious problems.	1 If you had allowed yourself four fixed times a day, reduce it to three and follow them religiously. Otherwise follow whatever times you have decided upon religiously. 2 At the end of the day record if reducing the number of fixed times to three caused you any serious problems.

15	16	17	18
1 If dropping to three times a day made no difference then stay at three; otherwise four times is for you. 2 Follow your set times religiously today.	1 If dropping to three times a day made no difference then stay at three; otherwise four times is for you. 2 Follow your set times religiously today.	1 If dropping to three times a day made no difference then stay at three; otherwise four times is for you. 2 Follow your set times religiously today.	1 If dropping to three times a day made no difference then stay at three; otherwise four times is for you. 2 Follow your set times religiously today.

22	23	24	25
1 If you're at three times a day, reduce it to two. At the end of the day record if doing this makes any serious difference. 2 Otherwise follow your set times religiously. 3 Resist the temptation to check emails 'just before I go home'. Whatever was your last set time should be just that.	1 If you're at three times a day, reduce it to two. At the end of the day record if doing this makes any serious difference. 2 Otherwise follow your set times religiously. 3 Resist the temptation to check emails 'just before I go home'. Whatever was your last set time should be just that.	1 If you're at three times a day, reduce it to two. At the end of the day record if doing this makes any serious difference. 2 Otherwise follow your set times religiously. 3 Resist the temptation to check emails 'just before I go home'. Whatever was your last set time should be just that.	1 If you're at three times a day, reduce it to two. At the end of the day record if doing this makes any serious difference. 2 Otherwise follow your set times religiously. 3 Resist the temptation to check emails 'just before I go home'. Whatever was your last set time should be just that.

29	30		
Follow whatever set times you have finally decided on religiously.	Follow whatever set times you have finally decided on religiously.		

5	6	7
Set your fixed times and follow them religiously.	Don't check emails – even if you have the capability at home to do so.	Don't check emails – even if you have the capability at home to do so.

12	13	14
1 If you had allowed yourself four fixed times a day, reduce it to three and follow them religiously. Otherwise follow whatever times you have decided upon religiously. 2 At the end of the day record if reducing the number of fixed times to three caused you any serious problems.	Don't check emails – even if you have the capability at home to do so.	Don't check emails – even if you have the capability at home to do so.

19	20	21
1 If dropping to three times a day made no difference then stay at three; otherwise four times is for you. 2 Follow your set times religiously today.	Don't check emails – even if you have the capability at home to do so.	Don't check emails – even if you have the capability at home to do so.

26	27	28
1 If you're at three times a day, reduce it to two. At the end of the day record if doing this makes any serious difference. 2 Otherwise follow your set times religiously. 3 Resist the temptation to check emails 'just before I go home'. Whatever was your last set time should be just that.	Don't check emails – even if you have the capability at home to do so.	Don't check emails – even if you have the capability at home to do so.

CHAPTER 5

Prioritising Viciously

There's prioritising and prioritising viciously. Let's take them in turn.

Prioritising

Sometimes you hear people say, 'I have five priority-one things to do, nineteen priority-two things and 37 priority-three things.'

That's not prioritisation.

Prioritisation is saying, 'If I could only do one thing on this list, what would it be?' Then that becomes your number-one priority. Then you take the remaining list and say, 'If I could only do one thing on this list, what would it be?' That's your number-two priority. And so on. You keep doing this, asking the same question until your list is prioritised. This is the only rule of the game. You're not allowed to have joint priorities – 15A and 15B – or something like that. Everything has to have an absolute priority.

The wife of the case study volunteer mentioned in the previous chapter also said this about her husband. 'Overweight – seriously. Smoker. No time to exercise. No time to eat properly.' If this man then asks the question, 'If I could only do one thing on my list, what would it be?', the answer has to be to get fit and healthy – eat properly, exercise, ideally give up smoking. If he doesn't then he may never get to do the other items on his list!

If you remember, this is my list from Chapter 2.

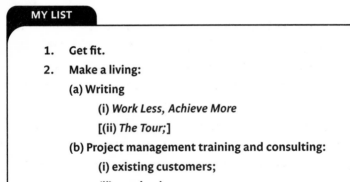

MY LIST

1. Get fit.
2. Make a living:
   (a) Writing
       (i) *Work Less, Achieve More*
       [(ii) *The Tour;*]
   (b) Project management training and consulting:
       (i) existing customers;
       (ii) new business.
3. Increase company revenue by 50%.
4. Learn a musical instrument.

Here's how I established the priorities:

1. Same as for the man mentioned in the previous paragraph. If I don't do this nothing else matters.

2. Make a living. Same as for most people. This book is now my top priority there. I have decided to do the first draft by writing 1,000 words a day for 60 days. The 1,000 words is now the first thing I do every day when I get up. If necessary I get up earlier in order to get time to do my 1,000 words. In the short term, the book doesn't contribute a lot of money to the cause of earning a living. In the long term it may.

3. Project management training and consulting is what really earns the money. It's my day job. Within that I have only two priorities – existing customers and new business, in that order. Notice that this order is probably true for anybody running anything that could remotely be classed as a business. (I include charities in this definition, for example.) You've got to take care of your existing customers first. If you could only do one thing it would be them. Without these you kill the goose that lays the golden egg. But then, after this – and it is, *after* this – you've got to be finding new customers. Otherwise your business may wither and die. Incredibly – even with a recession taking shape before our eyes – we're on target to do it.

4. Learn a musical instrument. Yep, I sure would like to learn but I'm just not getting to it at the moment. Some other stuff will have to go

because I don't have enough supply to match this particular demand. That's OK for now, though. Everything else is a 'must-do' for this year while learning the musical instrument is a nice ambition to have. As I've said earlier, I'm going to make a decision on which instrument this year, and then I will find the time for learning it next year.

I'm reasonably happy with these priorities. In a perfect world I wouldn't have to earn a living, and I'd be spending all my time getting fit, writing or learning an instrument. However, for the moment, I'm pretty happy with things the way they are.

Prioritising can be difficult

I accept that prioritising can be difficult. I think it can be difficult for two reasons. The first is that you're often not a hundred per cent sure about your priorities. Let me illustrate. When I first met Clare, my wife, she worked in a large multinational bank. About six months after I'd met her, she said, 'I've got my annual appraisal this Friday.'

(She had told me about the performance management system that her bank had. It was web-based, three-sixty-degree appraisal, everybody assessing everybody else, assessed by your peers, bosses and subordinates. They'd had consultants in – you know the kind of thing!)

'How are you going to do?' I asked.

(One of the ways I earn my living is by teaching short one-, two- or three-day training courses. I get assessed all the time. As a result, I need to have a fair idea, as I'm handing out the course assessment sheets – the so-called 'happy sheets' – at the end of the course, how I'm going to do.)

'I don't know,' she replied.

I started laughing because I thought she was kidding. But it turned out she wasn't. She didn't know how she was going to be assessed. She didn't know whether she'd be graded 'meets expectations' or 'exceeds expectations'.

I realised then that lots of people are in the same predicament. They don't know how they're going to be graded because they don't know *precisely* what their objectives are. They don't know the answer to the question, 'When the end of the year comes, boss – how will we both know that I've done the best possible job? Not just a good job but a really outstanding job.'

You need to be able to answer this question too for your job. It may take a bit of teasing out because many organisations and bosses seem to be more than happy to give out vague objectives like 'keep the customers happy' or 'bring the projects in on time and within budget'. But if you can get to a point where it's measurable – and my list in Chapter 2 would be a good example – then you're in business. In this case, your prioritisation should be much easier to do. It also should be said that there's no reason why anybody can't do this. It just takes a bit of teasing out with your boss.

The second reason that prioritisation can be difficult is that there is no space for shades of grey. You know the old expression, 'things aren't black and white'. Unfortunately, or fortunately perhaps, in prioritisation, things *are* black and white. One thing is either more important than something else or it is less important. There is no room for any middle ground; no third choice.

To help you then with doing your prioritisation, here's an intermediate step that you may find useful. (If not, you can head straight to the next section, but some people certainly find this a help.)

Take your list of priorities and, to the right of the list, rule two columns. Label one 'Frightfully important' and the other 'Other things'. (If it helps your thinking, you could label the second column, as somebody on one of my courses memorably did, 'Crappy little things'.)

Now run down your list and indicate by a tick which column each of the items on your list belongs in.

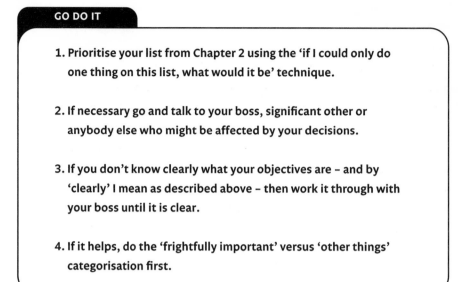

GO DO IT

1. Prioritise your list from Chapter 2 using the 'if I could only do one thing on this list, what would it be' technique.

2. If necessary go and talk to your boss, significant other or anybody else who might be affected by your decisions.

3. If you don't know clearly what your objectives are – and by 'clearly' I mean as described above – then work it through with your boss until it is clear.

4. If it helps, do the 'frightfully important' versus 'other things' categorisation first.

Prioritising viciously

Prioritising viciously takes prioritising a stage further. Here's how:
1. Do a Dance Card (Chapter 3) so that you not only have a list but also the amount of work (demand) in each item on the list.
2. Prioritise your list as before using the 'If I could only do one thing on this list, what would it be?' technique.
3. Draw a line across the list where supply = demand.
4. Do anything above the line; let anything below it go hang.

My list above is actually prioritised viciously. In particular this applies to the item 'Project management training and consulting'. I have only two priorities. Anything else can and does pretty much go hang.

GO DO IT

1. Take your Dance Card from Chapter 2 or do one if you haven't already.

2. Prioritise it using the 'If I could only do one thing on this list, what would it be?' technique.

3. Cut the list – draw a line – where supply = demand.

4. Put your time into those items above the line. Let the rest go hang.

'Bite the bullet' things

There are things that we put off. We put them off because they're unpleasant or boring or we're frightened of them. We're afraid of how much time they're going to take up; or we don't want to do them because we know it's pretty uninteresting work; or we're afraid of what the result is going to be – for example, a tax return; or we're afraid that we're going to make a mess of it – this would be me and a lot of DIY things; or we put it off because we don't like doing that kind of stuff anyway. And so on and so on. We put things off. As a result they languish somewhere on our priority list like Banquo's ghost at the feast.

For these you need to think in terms of them becoming a 'bite the bullet' thing. You probably know this expression. It means to endure pain with courage and comes from the time before effective anaesthetics had been invented. Soldiers were given bullets to bite on to help them endure pain, particularly during operations.

So, if you have one of these things – and who doesn't? – at some stage you need to give it bite-the-bullet status. This means that you are going to dramatically increase its priority. It means that today or this week or next Tuesday or whatever, that item is going to become your number-one priority. Nothing else gets done until it gets done.

It's the only way of getting those suckers off your list and consigned to history.

Another way to think about prioritising viciously

Stephen Covey talks about prioritising viciously in *The 4 Disciplines of Execution*. He describes it in a different way to me but the idea is the same. I mention it because what he says may resonate with you. This is the gist of what he says.

Some objectives are more important than others. Clearly then we should focus on these to the exclusion of others. We must figure out which goals and objectives are merely important and which are, what he calls, 'wildly important'. A wildly important goal carries serious consequences. Failure to achieve these goals renders all other achievements relatively inconsequential.

You can see then how this idea applies in my case. Failure to keep existing customers happy 'poisons the well' and the business is gone. Simple as that. Failure to find new customers means the business dries up and the business is gone. Equally simple as that. All the rest can (and does) wait or get dropped, ignored or sidelined in some way.

Prioritising viciously and saying 'no' nicely

I hope you can see the power of prioritising viciously and saying 'no' nicely, when combined. If you know what's really important then you know when to say 'no' to things. Something comes in and there's no agonising over it, no playing with it, no wondering whether you should do it or not, no tinkering and then dropping it and coming back to it again. Either it's important or it's not, i.e. either you intend to give this piece of demand some supply or you don't. If it's not important then forget about it – find a way to say 'no' nicely to it. If it is important, then it's either more or less important than other things so you can find a place for it in your day – using the A through D categorisation scheme. (See the last section of this chapter for a reminder, if you need it.)

Prioritising viciously and emails (aka Extreme email)

Look at how prioritising viciously helps with emails too. In your fixed times of the day to check emails, have a quick scan to see if there are any emails that relate to any of your really important things. If there are, you can give them an A and get to them. If there aren't, just ignore them. And I mean that literally – literally ignore them.

And do you ever deal with them? Well, you might. You could have maybe a 'bite the bullet' cleanup task when you try to get through them all. Alternatively you could delete them all. It's an extreme form of cleanup but it shouldn't be underestimated. I, for example, often do just that. This is extreme email management.

Prioritising viciously and going home on time

Let me tell you a story. In my last job working for somebody else, i.e. before I started my own business, I ran a foreign subsidiary of an American software company. Our subsidiary's job was twofold – to develop software products for our parent company and to support the European customer base. The company had a tradition of working long hours, pulling all-nighters, late-night meetings, working at weekends, bringing work home, burnout hours, all that kind of stuff. While the job was interesting and the work challenging – for the first couple of years anyway – that wasn't a culture that I subscribed to or wanted to reproduce at our location.

For a month or two I did the late-night thing and then I started going home on time. Let me be clear what I mean by this. I knew what my priorities were: (1) get software development projects completed on time and within budget, and (2) make sure the European customers were happy. Thus, if I had done what needed to be done each day to further these two objectives, then I would go home.

After a week or two of this my boss, who was based in the United States, started phoning me just before 5:00 p.m. In fact, to be completely accurate, what he started doing was getting his secretary to phone just before 5:00 p.m. and to say:

'_____ would like to speak to you.'

'No problem,' I would reply.

'Ah,' she'd say, 'but it's going to be a couple of hours before he can call you.'

I put up with this for a short while, hanging around waiting for him to call me. Finally, one evening, when she called and pulled this stunt, I said, 'Well, it'll take me about that long to get home. Can you get him to call me there?' (I lived a long way from the office which, in fact, was another thing he wasn't happy about.)

Eventually I won the 'going home early' battle. He was never happy about it. (Somebody met him recently – this is after twenty years – and evidently it still rankled. He still referred to me as 'the guy who came in last and went home first'. While the former was completely untrue – I was generally the one who opened the office – the latter usually was.) I continued to do it. We brought all of our projects in on time and within budget – something no other part of the organisation did – and kept the European customers happy. Our subsidiary was known as 'the part of the organisation that worked best'. I felt no guilt – or if I did, I expunged it fairly quickly.

Guilt occurs when we breach or violate a code to which we subscribe or pretend to subscribe. For a while I pretended to subscribe to the code of staying late. I wasn't happy doing it but I pretended. Eventually, I said, 'screw this' and dropped it. I felt happier, even if others didn't. But even if they weren't happy there was nothing they could do about it. This was because the code I subscribed to – doing the projects right and keeping the customers happy – was far more important to the organisation.

It's exactly the same for you. If you can find out what's 'wildly important' for you in your organisation, and focus on that, then a lot of other irrelevancies and dross fall away.

Here's another story that illustrates the same point. It was told to me by my father who was a salesman – apparently a great one. I never tire of telling this story. It describes prioritising viciously better than I ever will. I'll tell it as my father would have told it – larded with detail.

The sales manager is going through the department one day and he looks into the salesman's office. The salesman is there but he is not making phone calls, chasing up leads, doing his paperwork or anything else remotely related to his job. Instead he is sitting in his chair with his feet on the desk. He is carefully crafting paper planes and then flying them across the room. The ones that have landed or crashed are spread around the doorway of the salesman's office.

The sales manager storms in and angrily asks the salesman what the hell he thinks he's doing.

'Oh, bugger off,' comes the offhand reply.

The sales manager is outraged – nobody has ever spoken to him like this. He storms off to go and find his boss, the area manager. He explains to the area manager what happened. The area manager too is incensed. Together the two men go down to the salesman's office.

'Now, listen here,' says the area manager, as the two angry men arrive in the salesman's office. 'You can't speak to your manager like this. I believe you told him to bugger off. Is that true and if it is, what do you have to say for yourself?'

The salesman concentrates on completing a fold he is making in a new plane. Then he looks up, completely unconcerned, and says, 'Why don't you bugger off along with him?'

The area manager is apoplectic, speechless. As luck would have it, the area manager's boss – the regional manager – is visiting from head office that day. The sales manager and area manager find him and explain what happened. They're demanding an immediate sacking of the salesman. The three men – the sales manager, the area manager and the regional manager – go down to the salesman's office. As they enter, the regional manager has to duck to avoid getting a paper plane in the eye.

'I believe there's a problem,' says the regional manager.

'I don't think so,' says the salesman, picking up a fresh sheet of paper.

'But you told these two gentlemen to bugger off. You can't go round saying things like that to people. This is a very serious matter. What do you have to say for yourself?'

The salesman looks up at the regional manager and says, 'Would you ever go and take a long walk on a short pier?'

Stunned, the three men leave the office. The sales manager and the area manager are making noises about 'calling in Human Resources'. They look to the regional manager to see what he's going to do next.

'How are his sales figures?' asks the regional manager unexpectedly.

Surprised by the question, the area manager looks at the sales manager.

'Very good,' says the sales manager, 'he's way over target for the quarter. But that's hardly the point –'

'And the year as a whole?' asks the regional manager.

Again the area manager looks at the sales manager.

'Way over,' says the sales manager. 'He's a very good salesman.'

The regional manager turns and starts heading for the door. The two others scurry after him.

'Where are you going?' they chorus.

'I'm heading for the seafront,' he says. 'You two can make your own arrangements.'

As you have probably sensed, I *love* this story. It shows again how, if you know what your priorities really are, all other things fall away.

Is there a downside to prioritising viciously and saying 'no' nicely?

Thinking about it logically, then there has to be some kind of downside. Some things won't get done and this will mean some people aren't happy. But if you're doing the really important things then these people's unhappiness will be reduced to the level of quibbles. Then you're only left with two remaining issues – guilt and approval seeking.

Guilt you can deal with as described already. Stop subscribing to codes of conduct that you don't actually believe in. Put Frank Sinatra's 'My Way' on the stereo, play it loud and then do what it says. Be your own person.

And as for approval seeking, why do you care what other people think about you? If you're doing the wildly important stuff, then little else matters. They'll approve of that. And all the things they don't approve of? Well, those are all just their problems, aren't they?

Bringing it all together

In Chapter 2 I described how to use your daily list to get things done. (It's reproduced below, for your convenience.) Now see how:

• Prioritising viciously makes it child's play to know the As and Ds, and

• Saying 'no' nicely stops everything else from getting through.

These are the first two of our three filters working together. But we're not finished yet. There's one more to go which can again result in *vast* amounts of stuff not being done. It's called 'a little planning is better than a lot of firefighting' and is described in Chapters 6 to 10.

GO DO IT

> Carry on with the 30-day calendar from Chapter 2 but notice now that it should be even easier to be 'more vicious and strict and brutal' about the As and Ds.

The method for processing the daily list:

1. Look at your life list and see what things require some action by you today. For any that do, write what needs to be done on your daily list.
2. Look at your diary and see if there's anything else – appointments and suchlike – that need to go on to the daily list.
3. Ask yourself is there any other thing from any other source that might possibly need to be done today.
4. This list is your list of contenders – your list of things that could be done.
5. Now mark each item on the list with one of the letters A, B, C or D.
6. Here's what the letters mean:

   A: I have to get this done today. Planets will collide, stars will fall, bosses will be grumpy, share prices will nosedive if this thing isn't done. Be as vicious as you can about the As. Is it really that important? Why couldn't it wait? See also further comments below.

   B: It'd be nice to get it done today.

   C: Realistically I'm not going to get this done today.

   D: Delegate it. I can get somebody else to do this.

7. Do all the Ds first, i.e. get these items delegated.
8. Now do all the As.

9. When you're finished all the As, stop. Go home. Go on – go! Away with you! Off you go! What about the Bs and Cs? The answer is forget about them – they're for another day.

A couple of points. What happens if something new comes in during the day? Well then, what you do is add this item to your list and give it an A to D classification. Then you do it if it's an A or a D and leave it otherwise.

What happens if the end of the day comes and one of your As isn't done? Well then, it can't have been an A, can it? Notice when this happens and use this knowledge to make your classification of As more vicious and strict and brutal. You should soon get really good at it.

CHAPTER 6

A Little Planning is Better Than a Lot of Firefighting

In the end you have to do some things! Some things are important, i.e. align with your priorities and so make it down through the funnel. For these things you want to make sure that you do them with the least amount of effort. That's where planning comes in. Plan the work and work the plan, the old saying goes.

It will take us a few chapters to go through planning. That's not because planning is complicated – it isn't, though many people would have you believe that it is. Rather, it's that in order to get you to a point where you can do it instinctively and with as little effort as possible, I want to:

- Describe what you have to do;
- Justify why doing what you have to do is a good idea;
- Give you plenty of examples so that you can be in no doubt as to what is required.

Why plan?

When anything gets accomplished, it gets accomplished through a sequence of events. Whether it's something simple like making a cup of tea, or something incredibly large and complex like the Beijing Olympics, each is realised through a sequence of events. Planning is about trying to anticipate as much of that sequence of events as possible. Let me show you first why planning is smart and why there's actually no sensible alternative to it.

When you accomplish something, as we've said, it is through a sequence of events. There are essentially three ways to build this sequence of events. Let's look at them in turn.

The first way to build the sequence of events is to do nothing – to just let

Fate or chance build it for you. Here's what working on such an endeavour would be like. You'd come in in the morning and say, 'What'll I do today?' You'd work away on something and then you'd realise you needed something from somebody else. So you'd wander down the corridor or across the floor and find the guy and say, 'Do you have that other thing?' and he'd say, 'No, I won't have that until Friday.' And then you'd say, 'OK, I'll do something else,' and you would, and so the sequence of events would unfold and be built up.

It's ridiculous, you say. Nobody would do this. And yet I would bet my house and I reckon I would win the bet, that in your organisation today there are endeavours being run exactly like this. They are being run by Fate. This is happening not because people are stupid or incompetent but because people are too busy – they don't have enough time availability. They don't have enough supply for all the demand that they are committed to. They are multi-tasking, to use a popular term. If you find yourself in this lack-of-time-availability situation then this is exactly what happens – Fate takes over the running of your endeavours. If you're lucky these endeavours will end. On time and within budget? Pretty unlikely. Not when Fate lends a hand. So while many people adopt this approach – almost always inadvertently – it's a pretty lousy idea, I think you'll agree.

The second way to build the sequence of events is in real time. Here's what this is like. You come in in the morning and you have a to-do list and you start doing the first item on the list. But then somebody asks if you're coming to the nine o'clock meeting and then while you're at the nine o'clock meeting there's a knock on the door and somebody peeps in and says, 'Can I just get you for a moment?' and so you go outside to them and while you're talking to them your mobile phone rings so you answer that and you happen to be standing near your desk and your landline rings so you answer that just as your computer goes 'bing!' because an email has arrived and so you try to see what the email's about, talk to the person who pulled you from the meeting , answer your two calls, get back to the meeting...

You get the idea. You ricochet through the day. Gotta go here, gotta go there, do that thing, see that person, have that meeting... You may be familiar with the 'f' word – 'firefighting'. Building the sequence of events in real time is the idea that everything is a firefight; nothing could have been predicted. Now, I completely accept that firefights happen. On your endeavours and on mine, no matter how carefully they're planned, unexpected things happen. But not everything that happens on a project is a firefight. Many things could have been predicted if only we'd thought about them. And so, while many people adopt this method of building sequences of events, I think you'll agree it's hardly a smart way to do it. It's probably the recipe for a short, unhappy life.

That leaves the third and final option – planning. Or to put it another way, building the sequence of events at the beginning – before we undertake the endeavour. We will still have firefights – of course, we will – but then we can save our firefighting energy for the things that are genuine surprises.

If you're wondering why we should plan then, it seems to me that this is the answer – because there's no sensible alternative. If these are our three choices, then planning – i.e. building the sequence of events at the beginning – leaves the other two for dead.

What is a plan?

This is where people start to get a bit fretful. They think a plan, or 'a project plan' their boss may have said to them, scary!

It's not actually scary at all. A plan is five things:
- What – exactly – are we trying to do?
- What jobs do we have to do to get that thing done?
- Who's going to do those jobs?
- Who's going to keep the show on the road, i.e. who's going to run the plan?
- A safety margin – for when things go wrong.

Here's the plan for writing this book.

FIGURE 6.1

The plan for writing this book

ID	Info	Task Name	Duration in days	Start	Finish	Prede	Resource
1		1. Get Your Life Back	85	3/6/08	29/9/08		
2		1.1. 60,000 words @1,000 words a day @ 3 days per week	85	3/6/08	29/9/08		
3	✓	1.1.1. 1–10,000 words	5	3/6/08	9/6/08		Fergus
4	✓	1.1.2. 10,000–15,000	11.5	10/6/08	25/6/08	3	Fergus
5	✓	1.1.3. 15,000–20,000	4.5	25/6/08	1/7/08	4	Fergus
6	✓	1.1.4. 20,000–30,000 @ 5,000 pw	19	2/7/08	28/7/08	5	Fergus
7	✓	1.1.5. 30,000–40,000	18	29/7/08	21/8/08	6	Fergus
8	✓	1.1.6. 40,000–50,000	8	22/8/08	2/9/08	7	
9	✓	1.1.7. One third to Headline	3	3/9/08	5/9/08	8	
10	✓	1.1.8. Two thirds to Headline	3	6/9/08	10/9/08		Fergus
11	✓	1.1.9. Parts 1–5 to Headline	3	11/9/08	15/9/08	10	
12		1.1.10. Contingency	10	16/9/08	29/9/08	11	
13	✓	1.2 End	-	29/9/08	29/9/08	12	

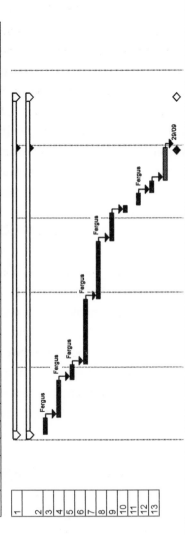

What are we trying to do? Write a 60,000 word book. What jobs have to be done? You can see them on the list, along with when they're going to get done. Who's going to do them? Well, no delegation here – I get to do them all! Who's keeping the show on the road? That's me, too – I'm the one who makes sure I'm making the deadlines and who changes the plan when things change. And finally, a safety margin? That's the line with the ID number 12. It's ten days to allow for things which might go wrong and which will still enable me to meet the deadline on 29 September. Finally, never mind that this plan appears to have been done using some kind of computer-based tool (it was!). The whole thing could just as easily have been done on a piece of paper, a wall chart or whatever. Remember the Egyptians built the Pyramids without paper, many wars were fought and empires won and lost using plans drawn up on bits of paper.

So – this is a plan. No big deal, eh?

What does a plan look like?

A plan can be represented in many different ways. The plan above is a so-called Gantt Chart (after the American engineer, Henry Laurence Gantt). It is one of the most popular ways of representing plans and is a who-does-what-when representation of the plan.

But another important representation is a spreadsheet showing a budget or a cashflow projection. A budget, for example, is a who-spends-what-when representation of a plan. We will see examples of both of these in the next chapter.

Should we use a plan for everything?

Sometimes one can get into a discussion about how big something has to be before you should build a plan for it. Does it have to be a 'project', some kind of formal initiative, for example? Should it be bigger than some number of man-days or have a budget greater than some amount of money? Here's my answer to this question.

Have you ever had this happen to you? Somebody comes running into you and says, 'This should only take you a couple of hours.' Two years later you're still working on it. If this has ever happened to you then you should consider doing a little plan whenever you're asked to do anything. It doesn't have to be a big production. Writing a book – as I currently am – is a big enough undertaking. However, you can see that the plan to do it is a fairly modest piece of work. It only took me a few minutes to put it together.

So should you build a plan for everything? For me, the answer is yes. The time spent doing it will always be rewarded by the time you won't have to spend firefighting. In fact, it's better than that. The time you spend doing a plan will be repaid many times over in terms of firefights you don't have to have. Or to put it another way, you will spend far less time firefighting than planning. Hence the title of this chapter.

So now we'd better talk exactly about how to build a plan. The next four chapters do exactly that as follows:

- What – exactly – are we trying to do? (Chapter 7)
- What jobs do we have to do to get that thing done? (Chapter 8)
- Who's going to do those jobs? (also Chapter 8)
- Who's going to keep the show on the road, i.e. who's going to run the plan? (also Chapter 8)
- A safety margin – for when things go wrong (Chapter 9).

There is then a fourth chapter (Chapter 10) which shows you how to execute that plan. Each chapter is structured the same way. It discusses the issues involved first. Then it gives the method – what exactly you must do. Finally, it gives an example.

CHAPTER 7

What Exactly Are We Trying to Do?

What – exactly – are you trying to do?

Many endeavours large and small go wrong because it wasn't clear to the participants what exactly they were trying to do. It may sound bizarre, unbelievable even. The truth is that it happens all the time.

Take the 1995 movie *Waterworld*, at one time the most expensive movie ever made, and one of the more infamous budget overruns in Hollywood history. This is a film where the script changed extensively during the filming. In other words, the makers didn't know exactly what they were trying to do even as they were doing it. Again, in the early nineties, The TAURUS (Transfer and Automated Registration of Uncertificated Stock) project at the London Stock Exchange was another example. By the time the project was abandoned, massively over budget and behind schedule, fundamental aspects of the design still hadn't been decided, i.e. not knowing exactly what they were trying to do. One could go on...

So you want to make sure this doesn't happen on your endeavour/ undertaking/project. (Let's agree that, for simplicity, we'll use the word 'project' from now on to cover any endeavour/undertaking/project. But let's agree too that 'project' can cover anything, ranging from something small – a few hours' work and involving just you – to something enormous with a cast of thousands.) How do you do this? How do you ensure that you know exactly what you're trying to do? There are two things you should do.

The first is to ask yourself the question, 'What event marks the end of this project?' It may seem like a trivial question but it isn't. Let me illustrate. Let's say your boss asks you for a new report on something or other. What event marks the end of this project? Well, maybe it's over when you come scampering into your boss with the report in your sweaty hand. But maybe that's not really the ending. Because if the report doesn't give her the right information or she'd like it presented a different way, then maybe you have to allow for some extra time to make these changes. And so the project isn't really over until you've made the changes, run it again and the boss is now happy with the result. But you could end up with two or three iterations before the boss declares herself to be happy with the report. So what event marks the end of this project? Well, in this example, any of the points I've described are possible endings. It's not that one of them is right and the others are wrong. The important thing is that you need to decide in conjunction with your boss so that there'll be no confusion or misunderstanding. You want to make sure you both have the same view of what constitutes the end. Otherwise there will be great unhappiness.

The second thing you must realise is that all projects affect people. Knowing who these people are and what they hope to get from the project is key to knowing exactly what it is you're trying to do. Often projects affect people whom we didn't expect to be affected in ways that we didn't expect. If that occurs then there's a fair chance that the project is already going – or gone – horribly wrong. So if you're to know exactly what it is you're trying to do, then you need to know (a) who's going to be affected, and (b) what these people expect to get from the project. The people who are affected by the project are often called 'stakeholders', for the simple reason that they have a stake in the project. Stakeholders are individuals or groups of people affected by the project. You need to know who your stakeholders are.

Furthermore, you need to know what they expect to get from the project. What individuals or groups of people hope to get from the project are often referred to as 'win-conditions'. Often we assume that all stakeholders have the same win-conditions as us. Things are almost never as simple as that. In general, different stakeholders have different win-conditions. If you fail to identify all of the stakeholders, or fail to identify their win-conditions, then your chance of delivering them by accident is pretty remote.

So, having figured out the end point of your project (as we described above) you need to see whether, when that end point comes, all of the stakeholders' win-conditions will have been met. How do you figure out the stakeholders' win-conditions? Well, the easiest way is to ask them. Here's an example.

I have two children – a 20-year-old son and an 11-year-old daughter, and if I ask them what they want to do for a summer holiday, I'm trying to establish the win-conditions of the stakeholders. We have three stakeholders in this example – me and them – and you can see how the win-conditions could be very, very different. I hope you can also see how crazy it would be for me to assume that what would be a good holiday for me would be a good holiday for them.

Here's another example. Let's say your boss asks you to run a job advertisement. Your department or organisation is looking for a certain type of person so your boss asks you to run an ad. Who are the stakeholders in this project? Well you and your boss, obviously. But hey, there are others, aren't there? The people who reply to the ad, the newspaper, the HR department in your organisation who, presumably, like to vet all the ads that are placed and who'll also have to look after the arrangements for processing all the applications, arranging interviews, 'no' letters, etc. There is also perhaps the sales and marketing department which wants to make sure the ad sends out a positive message about the company. Now, suddenly we're up to six stakeholders and the project is looking and sounding a whole lot more complex than just running a job ad.

The final thing to be aware of, when establishing exactly what you're trying to achieve, is to realise the following. Whatever it is you've been asked to do will probably change over the life of the project. It will change because:

- They (the stakeholders) will ask for some new things, or
- There will be something they asked for that you missed or didn't pick up on, or
- There will be something they should have told you about but they didn't, or
- There will be some change in the external (commercial, legal, regulatory, business) climate, or
- It may happen that, for example, they promise you five highly skilled team members for your project, but then take them for a more important project and send over a man and a dog to work for you!

Month by month, week by week, sometimes day by day, this is life on the project. There's no problem with this provided you don't let those changes happen in an uncontrolled way. Because here's the next big mistake that many people responsible for projects make. They assume that because they've committed to a plan/a budget/a schedule/a deadline for the project as it's initially given to them, then the people for whom they're doing the project – the stakeholders – can change their minds anyway they want, and the plan/the budget/the schedule/the deadline must still stand.

Now this is clearly nonsense, as a simple example will show. Let's say that the project you're asked to do is to 'make a container for water' and you believe that what you've been asked to make is a glass. Now it turns out, once the project gets rolling, that that's not really what they wanted. They wanted a jug – that's also a container for water. Now the plan/budget/schedule/deadline for making a glass are not the plan/budget/schedule/deadline for making a jug. But many project managers make the mistake of thinking that because they've committed to the initial ones, they must stay committed to them. (And if you're still not convinced by the glass and the jug, think of a glass and a swimming pool! These are both containers for water!)

You'd maybe have to ask how people running projects, who are generally fairly intelligent people, could make such a dumb mistake. The answer, it seems to me, has to do with the expression 'the customer is always right'. And yes, the customer is always right. The people for whom you're doing the project can change their minds any way they want. But every time they change their minds there's a price associated with that. There's a price in terms of money, or time or extra work. In controlling the changes we tell them the price. Some prices may be relatively trivial – they ask for a glass to be a little bit taller, for example. But some prices aren't trivial. 'We don't want a glass, we want a swimming pool' isn't trivial.

There's a more gut-level way to think about this whole business of controlling changes, and it's this. When a change occurs on a project, whether it's a small change like, 'Charlie's gone sick for half a day', or a very large change like, 'We don't want a glass, we want a swimming pool', there are only three possible ways to deal with the change.

The first way to deal with the change is that you can say to the stakeholders that this is a big change and is going to mean that they're going to have to agree to a new plan (budget/schedule/deadline). People sometimes refer to this as a 'change in the terms of reference' of the project.

The second way to deal with change is this. Many of the changes that occur on projects *aren't* big changes. They're the normal little 'woopsies' that happen on projects. For these we need to have contingency in the plan.

Finally then, in terms of dealing with changes, if:

- Something is a big change but we don't have the guts to say that to the stakeholders; and
- There's no contingency in the plan, either because we never put it in or we did, but then some genius took it out,

then we only have one other possibility and that is that we can 'suck it up', i.e. we can work more hours on the projects – nights, weekends, take work home with us, cancel personal plans, don't allow holidays during the project, etc.

On a healthy project all three options are available to us and are used. On an unhealthy project 'sucking it up' is the only thing that is done – a fact that, I think, most of us have had experience of.

So what do you do then? It is summarised in the box overleaf.

Now, let's see how we might apply this to an example.

Introduction to the Example

It's always a problem trying to decide what might make a good example to illustrate all of this. You need something that people can relate to, even that they might have to do themselves some day. But what are the chances that one can find something that will appeal to more than a tiny minority of readers?

I finally decided on the following. Many of the people that I spoke with in the course of writing this book – many of the case study people – were people who wanted to do something new. A lot of them wanted to start their own businesses or become self-employed in some kind of way. 'Start my own thing' was something that was on many people's minds. It seemed to me then that my example project should be to start a new business. Again, one is faced with the problem of *what* new business. How likely is it that two people will want to start the same business?

GO DO IT

1. Whenever you get handed a project or any kind of request, figure out what event would mark the end of this project.

2. Write down what would have to be done or achieved or delivered by the time that event takes place.

3. Make a list of all of the project's stakeholders. If your initial impression was that the request was pretty small and self-contained, yet your list of stakeholders is starting to grow, then maybe the thing isn't as simple as it may have first appeared to everybody.

4. Ask each of the stakeholders what their win-conditions are, i.e. what they would regard as a successful outcome to the project. Alternatively, write down what you believe to be their win-conditions, and then confirm those with them.

5. When the event that marks the end of your project is reached then all of the win-conditions need to have been met. (They don't all have to be met on that last day but they have to be met along the way.)

6. If it doesn't look like all the win-conditions are going to be met, then either the event that marks the end of your project needs to change or else some of the win-conditions need to change.

Here's what I decided to do in the end. I googled 'top ten new business ideas'. On a site called *www.entrepreneur.com* I found '10 Green Business Ideas'. That seemed like a good thing to do given the times we live in. From this list I took the one that appeared to require both the least money and the least specialist knowledge to start up. It was 'Green Cleaning Services'. Here's what the site said:

Cleaning homes and buildings can involve a multitude of chemicals that pose a risk to our health and environment. With people and businesses working hard to green their lives, there's a growing demand to have buildings cleaned without toxic or irritating chemicals.

While all buildings can benefit from green cleaning services, a particular niche for your business is the growing number of LEED [Leadership in Energy and Environmental Design]-certified buildings. Constructed using environmentally friendly materials, these buildings require special care. If cleaned in the usual way, the value of greening might easily be wasted.

Green cleaning avoids any chemicals that are skin irritants, toxic or harmful to the environment. Some cleaning services specialise in nothing but green cleaning; others provide it as a premium service. Going 100 per cent green helps capture the upper end of the market.

Currently no special certification is required to be an eco cleaner, although there are services that provide voluntary certification. Providing services beyond basic cleaning may help your green cleaning service stand out. For example, in addition to green toilet cleaning, how about fixing a leaky toilet to waste less water?

So there we are – you're going to start an environmentally friendly cleaning business. Now let's make some other assumptions to make the thing more realistic. Let's assume – just to make it a bit more complicated – you're in a full-time job at the moment. For now you're not ready to risk it all on this new venture, so you want to try it for say, a year and see how it goes. If at the end of that time it looks like it's a runner you'll then maybe do a plan to make it your new career. If not, you'll just keep it on as a sideline. So initially, your plan is going to be for one year. Let's begin applying our method. What exactly are we trying to do?

Example

As I write this it's 1 September so let's say that your plan is going to run from now until next 1 September. So if we ask the question, 'What event marks the end of this project', the answer is, 'Next 1 September'. When next 1 September rolls round then this project is done.

But what else? You want to have made some money by then. Let's say you would like to have six months' salary in the bank. This would then mean that you might be in a position to make this your full-time career, if you so choose. Then the six months' salary would act as your buffer and safety net.

What else would have to be done or achieved? Well, you'd want to have some satisfied customers. Since you are not going to be doing the home or office cleaning yourself, you're going to need a group of people to do that for you. You are going to have to have found a way of bringing in business. In broad terms, that's what you need to do.

Now, who are all of the project's stakeholders? Well, at first glance, they are (in no particular order):

- You
- Your dependants
- Your current employer
- Your customers
- Your cleaning crew

We can add the tax authorities and your suppliers and maybe that's pretty much it for the moment.

What are the win-conditions of each of these stakeholders? What would make a successful project for each of them?

You

The business is off the ground. You have customers, there's money coming in, you're paying your people and all your bills and taxes, you're building up your stash in the bank. Also – very important – your cleaning crew is happy; they are people you can trust and are not likely to try to run off with the business or start their own green cleaning business.

Your dependants

Your full-time job income stream hasn't been compromised in any way. Nor has your work/life balance been affected too negatively. Yes, this business is going to eat into your leisure time and so is going to take time away from your loved ones. But would it be possible, for example, to involve them? If you have children (of the right age), for instance, could they help with any aspects of it? Could they learn some useful business skills like marketing or sales or finance?

Your current employer
You don't (and your employer certainly doesn't) want your performance at work to be negatively affected by your new venture. Also you'll have to keep a very clear boundary between the two things. You can't be making cleaning-business-related calls from work, for example.

Your customers
They're happy with the service you provide and are giving you good references that you can use in your marketing and sales campaigns.

Your cleaning crew
They're happy.

The tax authorities
They're getting their share and they're happy.

Your suppliers
They're getting lots of orders from you and are being paid on time.

OK, let's go with that.

CHAPTER 8

What Do We Have to Do and Who's Going to Do It?

Once you've figured out exactly what you're trying to do, you then have to do what's known as *estimating*. This means you have to figure out what work has to be done, who's going to do it and a few more things besides.

There's only one problem: estimating is not just difficult – it's impossible!

There's an exercise we do on our training courses where we ask participants to do the following. We describe a series of tasks (a sequence of events) to them. We take one of those tasks and ask them to do a 'time estimate' for it. We tell them we will answer any questions they have to help them to do an accurate estimate. They generally ask lots of questions, all of which get answered. Despite this, when they eventually give their answers, there are huge variations between the smallest to the largest. (The smallest answer we've ever had to the exercise is half an hour and the largest is six months!)

How can one account for such a variation? Quite simply, the answer is that building and estimating this list of jobs is incredibly difficult. Since it basically amounts to predicting the future, we shouldn't be at all surprised at such variations. We are never going to get these lists and estimates 100 per cent accurate. The best we can hope for is to keep the error as small as possible.

Interestingly, this exercise also shows us how to deal with this problem. First of all, participants find that the more detail they can get about the task they have to estimate, the more accurate they will be. Second, there is a killer question which course participants almost never ask but which also would significantly help them. It is this: 'The last five times we did this task on projects, how long did it take?' These two factors – detail and what occurred in similar situations previously – are our two best guides when we try to build and estimate the list of tasks.

How we do all of this is the subject of this chapter.

Basics

At this stage, apart from identifying the jobs themselves, we usually also want to know a number of other things about each job. These are:

- How does this job relate to other jobs? Does it depend on another job finishing, for example? Can it run at the same time as some other job? These relationships are known as *dependencies*.
- How big is it i.e. how much *work* does it involve?
- How long will it take i.e. what is its *duration*?
- How much will it cost i.e. what is its *budget*?

A thing that causes people – even experienced people, who ought to know better – a lot of difficulty is the difference between work and duration. Let's define them and then give some examples so that you can be in no doubt about the difference between the two.

Duration, sometimes also called elapsed time, is *how long* a particular job is going to take. It is measured in the normal units of time – hours, days, months and so on. The normal duration of a soccer match, for example, is 90 minutes.

Work, sometimes called effort, is how much work is in a particular job. It is measured in units like man-days, person-hours, person-years and so on. The work in a football match, if we count two teams of 11, a referee, two linesmen and a fourth official is 26 times 90 minutes, i.e. 39 person-hours.

If you're primarily interested in *how long* a project is going to take, then duration is what you're primarily interested in. You identify all of the individual durations, string them all together, show what depends on what and what can happen at the same time, and this gives you the duration of the project.

But if you're interested in *how big* a project is or what it's going to cost, then duration won't tell you. For that you need work. You identify the work involved in each task, add all these up and this gives you the total size of the project. In addition, if you know everybody's daily rate you can figure out the cost of the labour (i.e. people's time) component of the project – one critical aspect of the budget.

Sometimes there's a relationship between work and duration – as there is in the football match example above – and sometimes there's no connection. One of the most common examples of that is where we say, ask somebody to review something. There may be half an hour's work in it but we give them, say, a week (duration) in which to do it.

Here are some further examples of work and duration so that you can start thinking in these terms. (If you're unsure about this maybe cover up the centre and right-hand columns and see if you come up with the right answers.)

WORK VS DURATION 1

EXAMPLE	WORK (EFFORT)	DURATION (ELAPSED TIME)
1. A meeting of six people lasting two hours	6 people times 2 hours is 12 person-hours	2 hours
2. Somebody reviewing some document or report for an hour	1 person times 1 hour is 1 person-hour	1 hour
3. Somebody reviewing some document or report for an hour but being given a week to come back with comments	1 person times 1 hour is 1 person hour	1 week
4. Somebody working for sixteen days full-time	1 person times 16 days is 16 person-days	16 days
5. Two people working full-time for eight days	2 people times 8 days is 16 person-days	8 days

And here's a different way to look at it.

WORK VS DURATION 2

WORK	PEOPLE'S AVAILABILITY	DURATION
1. 16 person-days	1 person working full-time for 16 days	16 days
2. 16 person-days	1 person working half-time for 32 days	32 days
3. 16 person-days	1 person working 1 day per week for 16 weeks	16 weeks
4. 16 person-days	2 people working full-time for 8 days	8 days
5. 16 person-days	2 people working half-time for 16 days	16 days
6. 16 person-days	2 people working 1 day a week for 8 weeks	8 weeks

So what do you do then? Our method is described in the next two sections. Notice that – almost inevitably – we're dealing once again with supply and demand. Demand is what jobs we have to do to secure the project and the amount of work in those jobs. Supply is the manpower to do those jobs.

Jobs and work

1. Get the people who will do the project involved in coming up with and estimating the list of jobs. If they're not all available, use those who are. If you don't know who these people are going to be, get somebody to help you. The worst thing you can do is to do this by yourself. Also there may be people with specialist knowledge about bits of the project. Involve them in the estimating or check estimates with them.
2. Identify the big pieces of work to be done in the project, the bits that get you from the start to the end. (Note that there are going to have to be chunks of work that ensure that each stakeholder win-condition is met. Win-conditions aren't met by accident!) You don't have to be too accurate or precise here. You're just trying to block out the big chunks of work that make up the project.
3. Where you do have to be precise is within each of these big pieces of work. Here, within each big piece, you have to identify all of the detailed jobs that have to be done.
4. Break everything down such that each job you identify is from 1–5 days' duration or 1–5 person-days of work.
5. Use cause and effect. Jobs don't exist in isolation. Once you write down your first job, then that job causes/triggers further jobs. Then each of those jobs causes further jobs. Use this idea to help you build sequences of jobs.
6. Be as specific and concrete as possible, i.e. rather than saying 'requirements gathering', say 'Charlie meets with the IT people for 2 days to explain his requirements'. Using simple language to describe jobs is a good way to ensure this. Write it so that a child could understand it! (There seems to be a great tendency to use fancy words

and phrases in plans. Try and avoid this temptation. The simpler it is to read and understand, the better.)

7. Where you don't know something, make an assumption. The problem with building these sequences of events is that we don't know all that we need to know about the project, i.e. we don't have enough knowledge. (The only day we have complete knowledge about the project is the day it ends – and then it's no good to us!) Assumptions are powerful because where we don't have the knowledge, i.e. have the facts, we make up the facts. If your assumption can be based on what happened previously, so much the better. In the absence of that, make a guess.

8. Write all the jobs down showing the project as being made up of the big pieces of work, which in turn are made up of the smaller pieces.

9. Add in one extra job called 'Project Management'. This will be to cover the time spent running the project, keeping the show on the road, allocating work, checking on things, sorting out problems and making sure things get done.

10. Now figure out how much work is involved in each job. Add all of these up to give the total work. To calculate the work involved in the 'Project Management' job mentioned in Step 9, calculate 10 per cent (one tenth) of the total work in the project. Add this to the total work to give the final total work figure.

11. Now figure out the duration of each job, when it can start and end and what other jobs it depends on or depend on it. For the 'Project Management' job show its duration running from the start of the project (the first day) to the end (the last day). This job doesn't depend on any other job – it runs parallel to all of them.

12. Notice finally that the total work number is an important number in all of this. This number is the sum of all the individual 'work' for each of the jobs. The work for a particular job is a measure of how much stuff has to get done. By adding up all of these we get a sense of the scale of the project – how big it is as a whole, how much stuff has to be done in this project. To get the project done there is going to have to be an equal amount of people-time available. Supply and Demand.

People to do the jobs

Now that you've identified what work has to be done, you must then find people to do the work. (People sometimes talk about 'estimating resource requirements' but this is really a rather silly idea. Once you know how much work has to be done, there's no estimation – it's arithmetic. If there are 100 person-days' worth of work to be done, there have to be 100 person-days' worth of people to do the work. Supply and Demand.

So now we must add two extra things to each job. They are:
- Who's going to do that job, and
- How much time that person has to devote to the task, i.e. are they available full-time, one day per week or whatever.

If you wanted to figure out the cost or budget for each job, this would be the place to do it. The cost of each job will by determined by two things. One is the work involved. For this you take the number of person-days that you have estimated and assuming that you know that person's daily rate, you can figure out the labour cost. The other thing is other costs – items like equipment, supplies, travel, subsistence, subcontractor fees and so on.

To make the method described in the previous two sections work there are three things you need to be conscious of. They are described in the next section.

Making the method work

In making the method work it is important for you to realise that you are building a sequence of events. This has the following implications:
- Each event in the sequence has to be crystal clear, i.e. it has to say exactly what is going on in that event. 'Charlie reviews the spec. for half a day with the two Marketing people' is crystal clear. 'Module F' isn't.
- There has to be cause and effect between the events, i.e. each event must lead to the next event.
- The events must be chained together.

So how do we do it then? What are the key questions we have to ask? It's very simple. They're questions like:

- 'So what's the first thing that happens?'
- 'Who does what?'
- 'And what happens then?'
- 'And then?'

If you ask these questions you'll always be able to build the list of jobs as accurately as possible. The next section shows the method and these ideas applied to Green Cleaning Services.

Example

What jobs have to be done?

Just a quick note before we start about how I've chosen to document this. For (my own) convenience in building this plan, I've drawn the plan for the project using a tool called Microsoft Project, a tool for planning projects. I've done this not because it's a particularly good or bad tool, or that you always need to use something like this, but merely because it will make the plans easy to read. When you come to do your own plans you can use what single tool or combination of tools works best for you. You can do your plan on paper (in a notebook or on flipchart pages), on a whiteboard or blackboard or some kind of wall planner, on your word processor, using a spreadsheet or you can use MS Project or some of its (freely available on the Internet) lookalikes.

The first thing our method says is to 'involve the people who will do the project in coming up with and estimating the list of jobs'. Let's assume that if you were doing this for real, you would involve some other people – your wife/husband/partner, for example, or a friend.

The next thing is to 'identify the big pieces of work to be done in the project, the bits that get you from the start to the end. Here they are – straight off the top of my head. Assuming you know nothing about environmentally friendly cleaning – and I don't – then you're going to have to find out something about it. This is because you'll need to be able to:

- Talk the talk to potential clients;
- Get a sense of the market and what prices you can charge;
- Explain things to your crew and be (or at least appear to be!) more

knowledgeable than them;
- Make sure that you get the right things from your suppliers and that they don't hoodwink you.

You'll need to find suppliers of products and equipment, a crew and, in particular, a trustworthy person to be in charge of the crew. You'll need to find customers and finally, you'll need to put the administrative and financial things in place.

So your top level plan is simply this:

TOP LEVEL PLAN

1. Research cleaning and green cleaning
2. Find suppliers of products and equipment
3. Find crew
4. Find customers
5. Administrative and financial stuff
6. Deliver the work

Next, our method says that you have to 'identify all of the detailed jobs that have to be done'. So what you do now is to take each of the big bits in turn and start to break them down further using the techniques we described above:
- Being as specific and concrete as possible
- Cause and effect
- Using whatever knowledge you have and, where you don't have knowledge, making assumptions.
  Here we go.

1 Research cleaning and green cleaning

You reckon a day spent on the Internet would enable you to find out enough about the industry to get you going. Since you've got your full-time job and you don't want to wipe out your work/life balance, you decide to do it over three evenings. This is what the plan shows.

Then you're going to check out some cleaning companies in your area to get an idea of pricing. Maybe some of this can be found online. It's more likely that you'll have to make phone calls and these will probably have to be done during office hours – so maybe you'll have to take a half day off to do this. You can do that during one of the three days – or maybe you'd be better taking a whole day off to do all of this. This is what you decide to do in the end. But you leave the plan showing three days since it may take a little while for some companies to come back to you.

Notice how, in doing this, you're starting to build a *realistic* plan. That's the trouble with a lot of plans – they have no basis in reality! Here, right from the word go you're starting to build a realistic chain of events.

That probably does it for '1. Research cleaning and green cleaning' for now. If we think of anything else we can add it in.

2 Find suppliers of products and equipment

Your research (job #1) will have told you what products you need. The plan that is now taking shape (in Figure 8.1 on page 110) shows that the next things you'll need to do are to make a shopping list of what you need and then go and buy the stuff. You'll put arrangements in place for regular resupply and this will maybe also enable you to get some volume discounts.

3 Find crew

You're going to need people to do the work and somebody really trustworthy to manage things on the ground. Let's say you decide that you're going to try and find part-time workers – maybe housewives/ homeworkers who'd like to make some extra money. For the foreman/ forewoman role you decide that the ideal profile would be somebody who maybe worked in some kind of supervisory capacity before, had stopped work – maybe to have children – and now wants to get back into the workforce. If s(he) had worked in the cleaning industry that would be even better.

For the workers you decide you'll advertise on community noticeboards in local supermarkets, community centres and so on. For the foreperson, you decide you'll use your local Jobcentre. You can see the possible sequences for these in the plan.

Notice that we haven't yet added stuff in like work and duration. We're going to focus on building the list of jobs. This is usually a good way to go about it – taking it one step at a time.

4 Find customers

This is probably where the bulk of your work is going to be. In broad terms you probably need to do two things:

- Decide what market you're going to go after – houses, offices or a combination
- Go and do some selling to find some customers.

Let's say that the following is what you decide to do. You decide you will initially target houses with leaflet drops. Because green cleaning would be seen as a bit of a premium or even luxury service, you decide you will focus on posher, upmarket areas where people would be more inclined (a) to get others to clean their houses and (b) to pay extra to get an environmentally friendly service. You decide on leaflet drops because they are relatively cheap to do and also because they can be done outside of your normal working hours. Your thinking is that once you've got a little customer base and a bit of a revenue stream, then you will start to go after offices.

In general, offices will require more of a 'sell' than houses. You will probably have to put your best business suit on and go and meet people and negotiate some kind of simple contract. However, the office business should help to ensure that members of your crew don't suddenly decide to go into the green cleaning business for themselves. House cleaning work is (you hope) relatively easy to find – the kind of stuff anyone could do. Fewer people (you hope again) would be inclined to start approaching offices and businesses.

You write some possible sequences of events into your plan. Notice too how building a plan enables you to make decisions like the house-versus-office one in a cool and unflustered way when there is little or no pressure on you. There will be pressures in the future. There will be firefights. Unexpected things will happen that you will have to respond to. But right now you can coolly navigate your way through your project. Notice finally that in building your plan, it is almost like you are building a simulation of your project and how it could evolve.

5 Administrative and financial stuff

Finally, there are some administrative and financial things you need to put in place. You'll need some kind of financial system to track invoices sent and payments to suppliers and crew. (You decide to use a spreadsheet on a computer you already have.) You'll need a bank account for your company. You'll need some kind of identity – business cards, headed paper, some kind of brochure when you start making office calls. Perhaps a presence on the web – and you could argue that these rightly belong up in the previous section on getting customers. And you'll need a contact point for people. You decide to buy a mobile phone and use it especially for this. You put some more jobs in your plan as shown in Figure 8.1 on page 110.

6 Deliver the work

Finally, you'll have to deliver any work you get. This will involve endless (you hope) repetitions of:
- Get a crew of one or more people there;
- With the necessary supplies and equipment;
- To do the job.

The final plan is shown in Figure 8.1. Never mind anything else in the plan for the moment except the jobs themselves and you can see where we have shown some dependencies between jobs.

FIGURE 8.1

ID	Info	Task Name	Work in days	Duration in days	Start	Finish
1		**1. Green Cleaning Services**	**31**	**4?**	**1/9/08**	**4/9/08**
2		**1.1. Research cleaning and green cleaning**	**3**	**3**	**1/9/08**	**3/9/08**
3		1.1.1. Learn the industry and get pricing	1	3	1/9/08	3/9/08
4						
5		**1.2. Find suppliers of products and equipment**	**1.5**	**2?**	**1/9/08**	**2/9/08**
6		1.2.1. Make a list of products and equipment needed	0.5	1?	1/9/08	1/9/08
7		1.2.2. Buy the stuff/put arrangements in place for regular supply	1	1?	2/9/08	2/9/08
8						
9		**1.3. Find crew**	**4.25**	**4?**	**1/9/08**	**4/9/08**
10		**1.3.1 Foreperson**	**1.75**	**4?**	**1/9/08**	**4/9/08**
11		1.3.1.1. Go talk to the Job Centre and find out how they can help	0.25	1?	1/9/08	1/9/08
12		1.3.1.2. Write job specification and give it to Job Centre	0.5	1?	2/9/08	2/9/08
13		1.3.1.3. Wait while they do their thing	0	1?	3/9/08	3/9/08
14		1.3.1.4. Interview applicants and choose one	1	1?	4/9/08	4/9/08
15		**1.3.2. The rest of the crew**	**2.5**	**2?**	**1/9/08**	**2/9/08**
16		1.3.2.1. Write advertisements for community notice boards	0.5	1?	1/9/08	1/9/08
17		1.3.2.2. As calls come in meet, interview and pick people	2	1?	2/9/08	2/9/08
18						
19		**1.4. Find customers**	**13**	**2?**	**1/9/08**	**2/9/08**
20		**1.4.1. House customers**	**1**	**1?**	**1/9/08**	**1/9/08**
21		1.4.1.1. Do leaflet drops in upmarket areas	1	1?	1/9/08	1/9/08
22		**1.4.2. Business customers**	**12**	**2?**	**1/9/08**	**2/9/08**
23		1.4.2.1. Do cold calls and get meetings	6	1?	1/9/08	1/9/08
24		1.4.2.2. Do meetings and get deals	6	1?	2/9/08	2/9/08
25						
26		**1.5. Administrative and financial stuff**	**6.25**	**1?**	**1/9/08**	**1/9/08**
27		1.5.1. Set up spreadsheet for tracking payments and income	1	1?	1/9/08	1/9/08
28		1.5.2. Set up bank account and buy mobile phone	0.25	1?	1/9/08	1/9/08
29		**1.5.3. Identity**	**6**	**1?**	**1/9/08**	**1/9/08**
30		1.5.3.1. Business cards and headed stationery	0.25	1?	1/9/08	1/9/08
31		1.5.3.2. Brochure	1.75	1?	1/9/08	1/9/08
32		1.5.3.3. Website	3	1?	1/9/08	1/9/08
33						
34		**1.6. Deliver the work – for each job landed do the following**	**5**	**1?**	**1/9/08**	**1/9/08**

The work involved in the jobs

Now we've got to figure out the *work* involved in each of the jobs. Why is this important? Well, it's important because work tells you how much stuff has to get done. Duration doesn't tell you this. Duration just tells you how long things are going to take. While, of course, this is important, I hope you can see the importance of knowing work. Let's say that when we calculate the work involved in setting up Green Cleaning Services, it comes out at 500 person-days. Then, given that there are about 240 working days in a year, it's not going to be possible to do it in your spare time – at least not in one year. You need to know work because work is the same as demand. Then, for the project to be successful, there has to be the same amount of supply as there is demand. If you don't know work (demand) you can't figure out how much of people's time (supply) will have to go into the project.

OK, on we go. We'll go through the items in our plan in turn and estimate the work involved in each of them. It's done in the following table and recorded in our plan in Figure 8.2 (see page 114). In Figure 8.2 we're only updating the 'Work' column at this stage. Notice too how assumptions play a part in helping us to do estimates.

THE WORK INVOLVED

JOB	WORK (IN PERSON-DAYS)	HOW IT WAS CALCULATED
1.1.1 Learn the industry and get pricing	1	We already said 1 day on the Internet plus contacting some other cleaning companies.
1.2.1 Make a list of products and equipment needed	0.5	Estimate half a day of additional research and making phone calls to suppliers to check availability and whether there are alternative products.
1.2.2 Buy the stuff/put arrangements in place for regular supply	1	This involves going round suppliers and picking up the stuff or arranging to have it delivered. Maybe also setting up accounts with suppliers. Let's assume that you can get everything you need from no more than three suppliers and that what will happen after this initial work is that they'll deliver to you.
1.3.1.1 Go and talk to the Jobcentre and find out how they can help	0.25	Assume a couple of hours out of your day to go to the Jobcentre and meet somebody.

CONTINUED

JOB	WORK (IN PERSON-DAYS)	HOW IT WAS CALCULATED
1.3.1.2 Write job specification and give it to the Jobcentre	0.5	Assume it takes half a day to craft it and get it right.
1.3.1.3 Wait while they do their thing	0	Doesn't involve any work from us.
1.3.1.4 Interview applicants and choose one	1	Assume that the Jobcentre comes up with, say, four applicants and you interview them over a day at the Jobcentre.
1.3.2.1 Write advertisements for community noticeboards	0.5	Assume it takes half a day to craft it and get it right.
1.3.2.2 As calls come in, meet, interview and pick people	2	Assume you end up interviewing ten people at 1.5 hours each and that you pick four of these. That's 15 hours – call it 2 (8-hour) days.
1.4.1.1 Do leaflet drops in upmarket areas	1	Assume a day to craft the leaflet and get it right. Assume you will do two drops a month; that's 24 in a year. Assume you will get your kids (or somebody's kids) to do the actual drops and that you will pay them per drop as opposed to quantifying their time.
1.4.2.1 Do cold-calls and get meetings	6	Assume 6 days of cold-calling over a year.
1.4.2.2 Do meetings and get deals	6	Assume 1 day's cold-calling is 100 calls and yields 1 meeting. (Sounds awful I know but that would be about right in my experience.) Assume the 6 meetings require proposals to be written. Assume half the proposals convert into deals. Assume half a day for a meeting and half a day to write a proposal. (First one might take a bit longer but after that, the first one should serve as a template for the others so that they can be written more quickly.)
1.5.1 Set up spreadsheet for tracking payments and income	1	Assume it can be done in a day.
1.5.2 Set up bank account	0.25	You'll probably have to go there in person rather than being able to do it over the phone or by email.
1.5.3.1 Business cards and headed stationery	0.25	Assume you go down to your local print shop to do it and that you pay them rather than counting their time.

CONTINUED

JOB	WORK (IN PERSON-DAYS)	HOW IT WAS CALCULATED
1.5.3.2 Brochure	1.75	Assume you do this yourself using your computer and a colour printer that you have.
Website	3	Assume you buy a book and do a simple website yourself using a lot of common content between the brochure and the site. Alternatively get your kid or his/her techie chum to do it and pay them.
Deliver the work. For each job landed, do the following: • Get a crew there (one or more people) • With the correct equipment and supplies • To get the job done	5	You make the big assumption that your foreperson is going to be able to do all of this. Maybe this means that it's a prerequisite for the job that they've worked in this kind of business before – or at least have some background in planning, logistics, that kind of thing. Notice again the value of building the plan and finding out this particular nugget. If you have to do all the organising of each job, you'll (a) give yourself a nervous breakdown and (b) probably end up being fired as your new venture takes over your life and your day job. This way your foreperson takes care of all this stuff –but then must be paid accordingly. So in terms of time what you have to count here is the time you will spend managing the foreperson. Let's assume that you decide to have a weekly meeting to review upcoming work for the week. Maybe you will do this some time over the weekend for the following week. Maybe the first few meetings will have to be face to face but after that some of them can be by phone or email with maybe just a fortnightly or a monthly face to face. Assume 52 meetings over the year, but lose a few for holidays (yours or theirs) – say 40 weekly meetings of no more than an hour each. Count your time because you're going to be paying them for theirs. 40 hours is 5 (8-hour) days.
TOTAL:	31 person-days	

So, in total, then, assuming you do it as you've described above, it looks like it will take about 31 days of your time over the next year.

Finally, don't forget that our method says that you also have to add in time for 'project management'. This is the time you will spend running the plan and making sure things happen when they're meant to. We said to use a rule of thumb of 10 per cent of the total work. In this case that's 3 person-days. So that's the next item that goes into the plan. Here's what your plan looks like now. Again – just to remind you – we've only done the jobs and the work so far, i.e. these are the only things that are correct in the plan.

FIGURE 8.2

ID	Info	Task Name	Work in days	Duration in days	Start	Finish
1		**1. Green Cleaning Services**	**34**	**4?**	**1/9/08**	**4/9/08**
2		**1.1. Research cleaning and green cleaning**	**1**	**3**	**1/9/08**	**3/9/08**
3		1.1.1. Learn the industry and get pricing	1	3	1/9/08	3/9/08
4						
5		**1.2. Find suppliers of products and equipment**	**1.5**	**2?**	**1/9/08**	**2/9/08**
6		1.2.1. Make a list of products and equipment needed	0.5	1?	1/9/08	1/9/08
7		1.2.2. Buy the stuff/put arrangements in place for regular supply	1	1?	2/9/08	2/9/08
8						
9		**1.3. Find crew**	**4.25**	**4?**	**1/9/08**	**4/9/08**
10		**1.3.1 Foreperson**	**1.75**	**4?**	**1/9/08**	**4/9/08**
11		1.3.1.1. Go talk to the Job Centre and find out how they can help	0.25	1?	1/9/08	1/9/08
12		1.3.1.2. Write job specification and give it to Job Centre	0.5	1?	2/9/08	2/9/08
13		1.3.1.3. Wait while they do their thing	0	1?	3/9/08	3/9/08
14		1.3.1.4. Interview applicants and choose one	1	1?	4/9/08	4/9/08
15		**1.3.2. The rest of the crew**	**2.5**	**2?**	**1/9/08**	**2/9/08**
16		1.3.2.1. Write advertisements for community notice boards	0.5	1?	1/9/08	1/9/08
17		1.3.2.2. As calls come in meet, interview and pick people	2	1?	2/9/08	2/9/08
18						
19		**1.4. Find customers**	**13**	**2?**	**1/9/08**	**2/9/08**
20		**1.4.1. House customers**	**1**	**1?**	**1/9/08**	**1/9/08**
21		1.4.1.1. Do leaflet drops in upmarket areas	1	1?	1/9/08	1/9/08
22		**1.4.2. Business customers**	**12**	**2?**	**1/9/08**	**2/9/08**
23		1.4.2.1. Do cold calls and get meetings	6	1?	1/9/08	1/9/08
24		1.4.2.2. Do meetings and get deals	6	1?	2/9/08	2/9/08
25						
26		**1.5. Administrative and financial stuff**	**6.25**	**1?**	**1/9/08**	**1/9/08**
27		1.5.1. Set up spreadsheet for tracking payments and income	1	1?	1/9/08	1/9/08
28		1.5.2. Set up bank account and buy mobile phone	0.25	1?	1/9/08	1/9/08
29		**1.5.3. Identity**	**6**	**1?**	**1/9/08**	**1/9/08**
30		1.5.3.1. Business cards and headed stationery	0.25	1?	1/9/08	1/9/08
31		1.5.3.2. Brochure	1.75	1?	1/9/08	1/9/08
32		1.5.3.3. Website	3	1?	1/9/08	1/9/08
33						
34		**1.6. Deliver the work – for each job landed do the following**	**5**	**1?**	**1/9/08**	**1/9/08**
35						
36		**1.7. Project Management**	**3**	**1?**	**1/9/08**	**1/9/08**

The next thing you've got to figure out is when things are going to happen and what depends on what.

When things are going to happen and what depends on what

Once again we'll go through the tasks one by one and now look at when they can happen, how long they're going to take and on what other things they're going to depend. We'll add these durations to the plan (see Figure 8.3 on page 118).

TASKS AND DURATION

JOB	WORK (IN PERSON-DAYS)	HOW IT WAS CALCULATED
1.1.1 Learn the industry and get pricing	1	You decide to give the whole thing a kick-start by taking a week off out of your holiday entitlement to get the ball rolling. This means that for that week you can work full-time on tasks, i.e. your availability is full-time.
1.2.1 Make a list of products and equipment needed	0.5	You do this during that first week.
1.2.2 Buy the stuff/put arrangements in place for regular supply	1	You don't really want to do this until closer to the time when you have your crew in place. You do it one Saturday during the time that the Jobcentre is waiting for foreperson applications to come in and you're waiting for replies from community noticeboards.
1.3.1.1 Go and talk to the Jobcentre and find out how they can help	0.25	You do this during that first week.
1.3.1.2 Write job specification and give it to the Jobcentre	0.5	You do this during that first week.
1.3.1.3 Wait while they do their thing	20	The Jobcentre says that they'll allow four weeks for applications to come in for the foreperson's job.
1.3.1.4 Interview applicants and choose one	1	You decide you'll have to take another day off to interview the applicants for the foreperson's job. Since you don't have infinite holiday entitlements and you do actually want to take some holidays as holidays, you revise your original idea to take 5 days off in one block. You decide to take 4 of them now and 1 to do the

JOB	WORK (IN PERSON-DAYS)	HOW IT WAS CALCULATED
		foreperson job interviews when that time comes round. Note yet again the value of this type of planning. If you hadn't done this there would have been some kind of crisis when the Jobcentre called up and asked, 'When would you like to interview these people we've got for you?' This way, the issue is already taken care of.
1.3.2.1 Write advertisements for community noticeboards	0.5	You do this during that first week.
1.3.2.2 As calls come in, meet, interview and pick people	20	You decide you'll interview people in the evenings and at weekends. After this initial crop of people, you decide it will be the foreperson's job to hire any new people for the crew. You add this very important fact which you've just learned to the foreperson's job description.
1.4.1.1 Do leaflet drops in upmarket areas	5	You can see from the plan that everything is ready to roll by 2 October. So perhaps the week before this you do your first leaflet drop. Then they'll happen every two weeks after that. For clarity, I've just shown the first one on the plan. You give the kids a week in which to get it done.
1.4.2.1 Do cold-calls and get meetings		You decide you won't start doing these until the new year when you've built up a bit of experience, have made mistakes, have a bit of a track record and have some satisfied customers who can give you references. You make a note to yourself to ask for such references at the conclusion of each job and also to ask your home cleaning customers whether they might have leads into businesses. If it's the posh part of town then presumably there are business owners there. However, these will form no further part of this plan.
1.4.2.2 Do meetings and get deals		See previous comment.
1.5.1 Set up spreadsheet for tracking payments and income	1	You do this during that first week.
1.5.2 Set up bank account	0.25	You do this during that first week. That's your initial 4 days' holiday gone.
1.5.3.1 Business cards and headed stationery	1	You're going to do this on a regular working day during your lunch break.
1.5.3.2 Brochure	7	You're going to work on this at nights, a couple of hours a night (i.e. a quarter of a day every night). At that rate it will take 7 days.

CONTINUED

JOB	WORK (IN PERSON-DAYS)	HOW IT WAS CALCULATED
Website	12	Similarly for the website which you decide to do yourself. It will take you 12 days (at a quarter of a day every night).
Deliver the work.		Here's how it will all work. The (hopefully, lots of) calls will come into your mobile phone. Since you will probably be at work when this happens, you will have to call them back. There will be a message on your phone that says that.
		When you call them back, you will figure out what they want and price the work. If you get the deal then you will then pass the job on to the foreperson who will schedule the crew and do the work.
		There remains the sticky question of how you get paid. You decide eventually that you have no real choice. The homeowner will pay the money to the foreperson and you'll collect the money off the foreperson at the weekly meeting.
		This means the foreperson will know exactly how much you're making, increasing the likelihood that they might start their own green cleaning services. But for the moment, you're going to have to live with that.

FIGURE 8.3

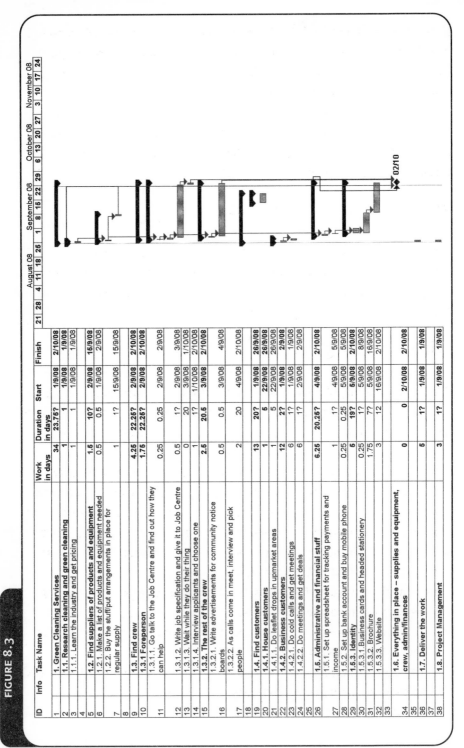

ID	Info	Task Name	Work in days	Duration in days	Start	Finish
1		1. Green Cleaning Services	34	23.762	1/9/08	2/10/08
2		1.1. Research cleaning and green cleaning	1	1	1/9/08	1/9/08
3		1.1.1. Learn the industry and get pricing	1	1	1/9/08	1/9/08
4						
5		1.2. Find suppliers of products and equipment	1.5	107	2/9/08	16/9/08
6		1.2.1. Make a list of products and equipment needed	0.5	0.5	1/9/08	2/9/08
7		1.2.2. Buy the stuff/put arrangements in place for regular supply	1	17	15/9/08	15/9/08
8						
9		1.3. Find crew	4.25	22.267	2/9/08	2/10/08
10		1.3.1 Foreperson	1.75	22.267	2/9/08	2/10/08
11		1.3.1.1. Go talk to the Job Centre and find out how they can help	0.25	0.25	2/9/08	2/9/08
12		1.3.1.2. Write job specification and give it to Job Centre	0.5	17	2/9/08	3/9/08
13		1.3.1.3. Wait while they do their thing	0	20	3/9/08	1/10/08
14		1.3.1.4. Interview applicants and choose one	1	17	1/10/08	2/10/08
15		1.3.2. The rest of the crew	2.5	20.5	3/9/08	2/10/08
16		1.3.2.1. Write advertisements for community notice boards	0.5	0.5	3/9/08	4/9/08
17		1.3.2.2. As calls come in meet, interview and pick people	2	20	4/9/08	2/10/08
18						
19		1.4. Find customers	13	207	1/9/08	26/9/08
20		1.4.1. House customers	1	6	22/9/08	26/9/08
21		1.4.1.1. Do leaflet drops in upmarket areas	1	5	22/9/08	26/9/08
22		1.4.2. Business customers	12	27	1/9/08	2/9/08
23		1.4.2.1. Do cold calls and get meetings	6	17	1/9/08	1/9/08
24		1.4.2.2. Do meetings and get deals	6	17	2/9/08	2/9/08
25						
26		1.5. Administrative and financial stuff	6.25	20.267	4/9/08	2/10/08
27		1.5.1. Set up spreadsheet for tracking payments and income	1	17	4/9/08	5/9/08
28		1.5.2. Set up bank account and buy mobile phone	0.25	0.25	5/9/08	5/9/08
29		1.5.3. Identity	5	19?	5/9/08	2/10/08
30		1.5.3.1 Business cards and headed stationery	0.25	17	5/9/08	8/9/08
31		1.5.3.2. Brochure	1.75	77	5/9/08	16/9/08
32		1.5.3.3. Website	3	12	16/9/08	2/10/08
33						
34		1.6. Everything in place – supplies and equipment, crew, admin/finances	0	0	2/10/08	2/10/08
35						
36		1.7. Deliver the work	5	17	1/9/08	1/9/08
37						
38		1.8. Project Management	3	17	1/9/08	1/9/08

Notice that we don't total the duration column. It would only be correct to do this if all of the jobs happened in sequence, one after the other. But since things happen in parallel with one another in our plan, totalling this column wouldn't make any sense.

Now we know how much work is involved and how long things are going to take. In particular we know the demand – 34 person-days. Now where's the supply going to come from and what's it going to cost? We answer these questions in the next two sections.

Who's going to do the jobs?

Well, that's easy really. You and the foreperson are the two main contributors. You're going to put in 34 person-days of your time to get everything set up and to monitor the foreperson via the weekly meetings. They'll run the day-to-day operations.

What's it going to cost?

The first cost is the 34 person-days of your time. Entrepreneurs call this 'sweat capital'. It's generally regarded as being free! The costs where you'll have to shell out money – cold, hard cash – are shown in the following table. I've assumed the currency is euros.

Also notice that so far you've represented your plan as a Gantt Chart. The best way to represent the what's-it-going-to-cost aspect of the plan is with a spreadsheet. The spreadsheet will show when you have to pay out money and when it's going to come in. This view of the plan is going to be your key tool in the survival or otherwise of your business. Figure 8.4 (see page 121) shows that view of the plan.

Note finally that some further assumptions have been made regarding volumes and timing of work and these are as follows:

1. You already have your own computer, software and colour printer so there is no cost associated with these.
2. You decide that, for the first year, you won't set up a limited company so there are no legal, accountancy or audit fees.
3. You don't land any work in September.

4. You get a bit of a boost around Christmas when more people want their houses cleaned.
5. The initial load of supplies you get keeps you going for two months.
6. The deals you land in the other months represent house deals only. Any office deals you might land are not shown.
7. Other assumptions regarding pricing are shown in the spreadsheet.
8. We assume that we charge an average 4-hour job at €120.

COSTINGS

JOB	COST (IN EUROS)	HOW IT WAS CALCULATED
1.2.2 Buy the stuff/put arrangements in place for regular supply	500	An assumption (guess!) until you can go and talk to the suppliers.
1.4.1.1 Do leaflet drops in upmarket areas	960	You'll have to pay the kids. Two kids at say, €20 each per drop. That's 2 x 20 x 24 = €960. But in the first September you'll just do one drop, so that's €920.
1.5.2 Mobile phone	1,200	Assume it's a pay-as-you-go phone and that the cost will be €100 per month.
1.5.3.1 Business cards and headed stationery	100	Say €100
1.5.3.2 Brochure	0	You decide to do this using your own computer, software and colour printer, so the cost is nil.
1.5.3.3 Website	130	You do this too so the cost is the €30 you're going to pay for a book about how to do it. There's also going to be the cost of the website and web hosting. Say another €100.
1.6 Deliver the work	See spreadsheet in Figure 8.4	Assume you're going to pay your foreperson €15 per hour and your crew €10 per hour. Assume that your foreperson will have to invest an average of an hour in a typical house job – organising to get the crew there, getting supplies to the crew and then picking up the money. Assume one crew member can do a reasonably sized house in 4 hours. Sure, jobs will vary depending on the size of the house, what needs doing, etc. but I have it on good authority from somebody who's done this kind of work that 'a lot could be done in four hours'. Assume initially, everyone will just work on demand, i.e. nobody will be on any kind of salary. If there's no work, nobody gets paid. Notice again the value of involving other people in doing estimating – particularly people with specialist knowledge.

FIGURE 8.4: GREEN CLEANING SERVICES – 1-YEAR PLAN IN FINANCIAL FORM

All amounts in euros

Expenditure

	Sep	Oct	Nov	Dec	Jan	Feb	Mar	Apr	May	Jun	Jul	Aug	TOTALS
1.2.2 Equipment and supplies (initial, further)	500			200	200	200	200	200	200	200	200	200	2,300
1.4.1.1 Leaflet drops	40	80	80	80	80	80	80	80	80	80	80	80	920
1.5.2 Phone	25	50	50	50	75	75	75	100	100	100	100	100	900
1.5.3.1 Business cards and headed stationery	100												100
1.5.3.3 Book & website hosting	100												100
Number of houses	0	2	4	8	6	8	10	12	14	16	18	20	118
Wages foreperson and crew	0	102	204	408	306	408	510	612	714	816	918	1,020	6,018
Total expenditure	765	234	338	746	667	771	875	1,004	1,108	1,212	1,316	1,420	10,456
Income / revenue	0	240	480	960	720	960	1200	1440	1680	1920	2160	2400	14,160
PROFIT / LOSS	-765	6	142	214	53	189	325	436	572	708	844	980	3,704

ASSUMPTIONS

Number of leaflet drops per month:	2 (except for the first September which is only one)		
Cost of a leaflet drop:	40 €		
Monthly cost of supplies:	200 €		
Average foreperson time on a house	1 hour	Wages foreperson	15 per hour
Average crew time on a house	4 hours	Wages crew	9 per hour
Total wages to do a house	51		
Cost charged for a typical 4-hour job	120		

The plan as a simulation of the project

We've mentioned this already, about being able to use the plan as a simulation of the project. Looking again at Figure 8.4 we can see how this representation of the plan can help us to explore options and make decisions.

To begin with, the profit level doesn't seem that high. Maybe you've got too many leaflet drops going on given that you've been reasonably conservative about the number of jobs you're going to land. So supposing you assumed you landed double the number of jobs per leaflet drop, what would that do to the plan? It makes a big difference as shown in Figure 8.5.

Given that the wages part of your costs can't really be changed – it's minimum wage for the crew and a bit more for the foreperson – then the key to making this business profitable is going to be lots of jobs. That means more leaflet drops, not less. And it also means that the push to get office business should come sooner because these jobs will be bigger in size and value.

Furthermore, one of the biggest expenses there is the foreperson. If you didn't have that person and did the work yourself, your plan shows you what you would be earning. Would that work for you and would it be enough to risk giving up your day job? Or maybe it's better to remember that everything in your plan is just a prediction at the moment. Maybe better to see what happens in reality for a few months, how closely what actually happens compares with what you predicted. Then you can make the call to jump ship or not.

Enough! But you get the idea. These are just some of the things you can explore with your plan.

GO DO IT

Once you've figured out exactly what your project is meant to deliver, as described in Chapter 7, then build a plan for your project as described above.

FIGURE 8.5: GREEN CLEANING SERVICES – 1-YEAR PLAN IN FINANCIAL FORM WITH DOUBLE THE DEALS

All amounts in euros

Expenditure	Sep	Oct	Nov	Dec	Jan	Feb	Mar	Apr	May	Jun	Jul	Aug	TOTALS
1.2.2 Equipment and supplies (initial, further)	500			200	200	200	200	200	200	200	200	200	2,300
1.4.1.1 Leaflet drops	40	80	80	80	80	80	80	80	80	80	80	80	920
1.5.2 Phone	25	50	50	50	75	75	75	100	100	100	100	100	900
1.5.3.1 Business cards and headed stationery	100												100
1.5.3.3 Book & website hosting	100												100
Number of houses	0	4	8	15	12	16	20	24	28	32	36	40	235
Wages foreperson and crew	0	204	408	765	612	816	1,020	1,224	1,428	1,632	1,836	2,040	11,985
Total expenditure	765	338	546	1,110	979	1,187	1,395	1,628	1,836	2,044	2,252	2,460	16,540
Income / revenue	0	480	960	1800	1440	1920	2400	2880	3360	3840	4320	4800	28200
PROFIT / LOSS	-765	142	414	690	461	733	1,005	1,252	1,524	1,796	2,068	2,340	11,660

ASSUMPTIONS

Number of leaflet drops per month:	2 (except for the first September which is only one)	
Cost of a leaflet drop:	40 €	
Monthly cost of supplies:	200 €	
Average foreperson time on a house:	1 hour	Wages foreperson 15 per hour
Average crew time on a house:	4 hours	Wages crew 9 per hour
Total wages to do a house:	51	
Cost charged for a typical 4 hour job:	120	

CHAPTER 9

What If Things Go Wrong?

A safety margin – for when things go wrong

We've already said that we can't get our estimates 100 per cent right. In addition we know that unexpected stuff happens on projects. Most of it is *bad* unexpected stuff, in the sense that it will have a negative effect on the project. So for these two reasons we need to have a safety margin or a margin for error in the plan. We'll look at two ways of doing that – contingency and risk analysis – a belt and braces approach to the safety margin on our project.

Contingency

The first thing to be said about contingency is that it's mandatory. You really have to have it. If you don't then you lose one of your three possible responses to change that we spoke about in Chapter 7. If you have no contingency on your project then every change that occurs on your project, which is not a big change, will have to be dealt with by sucking it up, i.e. by working more hours. And lots of the things that happen on projects aren't big changes. To condemn yourself and your team to working more hours to deal with changes is a really bad idea, I think you'll agree.

There are some industries and sectors where people expect to see contingency in a plan – sectors like construction, for example, or film-making. Then there are other sectors – the one I came from, software development, is a perfect example – where if people (bosses and/or stakeholders) see contingency in a plan, they often have a tendency to draw a red line through it and say, 'Well, that can go for starters.'

If you believe this is going to happen to you on your particular project or with your particular stakeholders, then the next decision you need to make is whether to put contingency explicitly in plans or to hide it. There is an argument that says you put it in explicitly *and* you hide it. You still have it in there, your boss or stakeholders get the satisfaction of taking it out and, if you stop them from taking it out you have twice as much – and you won't get any arguments from me on that score.

If you next ask the question, 'How much contingency should I have in my plan?', then the answer, in general, is, 'As much as you can get away with.' So if you then say to me, 'Fifty per cent?' I'll say, 'Yes, if you can get away with it.' 'One hundred per cent?' Sure – if you could, because the more contingency you have, the greater the likelihood that the prediction you're making is going to come true. And before you ask about what this will do to the project's momentum, let's get real and recognise that you won't get 50 or 100 per cent, of course. Typically, contingency in plans ends up about 10 to 15 per cent of the project duration or the project resources or the project budget.

Here are two easy ways to put contingency in your plan. They're not the only two ways, but they're two that are simple, easy when it comes to tracking the project and which work well together. The first is to realise that in almost every project, some bits are more important than others. (Sure, some projects are all or nothing projects – the changeover to the euro, for example, or the Year 2000 computer problem, but by and large, these are the exception.) If you can separate the things your project is delivering into have-to-have and nice-to-have, you'll be far better off than if you just say that you're going to deliver everything.

Plan to deliver the have-to-have first. This will enable the stakeholders to start using whatever it is the project has delivered, enable them to start solving some of the problems the project was meant to solve, trying out whatever it is and finding any problems with it. It gives you early feedback on what you've done and also takes the heat off you in terms of delivery.

Another variant on this is some sort of phased or incremental delivery where you roll out the project to the stakeholders in phases or increments. 'Under-promise and over-deliver,' the old saying goes. Doing some form of phased or incremental delivery as we have just described enables you to do exactly this.

The other way to put contingency in your plan is to add on some extra time. Anyone who has ever added on some extra time to a journey time, 'just to be on the safe side', will be familiar with this. Let's say that your basic plan tells you that the project will be done by 10 August; then you tell the stakeholders 31 August. You tell the team that they must be done by 10 August. If they get to August and they're done, then they can go to the beach for the next three weeks. If they get to 10 August and they're not done then the extra time you're going to negotiate with the stakeholders may save your collective bacon. It's important that they focus on 10 August though. Otherwise, if they start thinking in terms of 31 August, then essentially your contingency evaporates.

Risk Analysis

Contingency assumes that, irrespective of how well we plan, bad stuff will happen on our project. (And it will!) Risk Analysis tries to stop some of these bad things from happening. It does this by:
- Identifying the things most likely to affect the project (risks = threats = banana skins)
- Grading these according to their likelihood and potential impact
- Taking actions to deal with the most severe threats.

Here's how to do that.

RISKS

Likelihood: *On a scale of 1–3 where 1 = low likelihood, 3 = high likelihood and 2 = anything else.*

Impact: *On a scale of 1–3 where 1 = low impact, 3 = high impact and 2 = anything else.*

Exposure: *Found by multiplying the Likelihood by the Impact – a number between 1 and 9; the higher the number the greater the risk.*

Actions: *Jobs we can carry out (which should go into the list of jobs) to reduce or eliminate the risks whose exposure is 6 or 9.*

Any risks that get a rating of 6 or a 9 for Exposure need to be looked at. Anything else can be ignored. Note that the 'Actions' (in the final column) are jobs which should end up back in the list of jobs and be done the same way as any other jobs.

Example

I hope you can see that there are a few ways that you have put contingency into the Green Cleaning Services plan. There is no full-time staff, for example, so if it all goes horribly wrong you won't have to make people redundant or pay severance packages. There is very little hard cash investment. And what's there could be further reduced by a lower upfront purchase of supplies and equipment and delaying the business cards and stationery. The number of leaflet drops can also be scaled back if the idea doesn't look like taking off.

The plan as we've drawn it up doesn't require you to quit your day job – something entrepreneurs often have to do. So, all in all, it's a very 'safe', low-risk plan.

In terms of a risk analysis, here's what it might look like:

RISK ANALYSIS

	Risk	L	I	E	Actions
1	Can't get supplies and products	1	1	1	
2	Can't get staff	1	3	3	
3	Customers aren't interested	2	3	6	Don't give up too soon; set a limit on how much time, effort and money you are prepared to invest in it.
4	Can't find kids to do leaflet drops	1	3	3	
5	Don't have enough money to start	2	3	6	Get a bank loan or an overdraft for, say, €1,000. That gives you a little bit of contingency.

GO DO IT

Add contingency to your plan and do a risk analysis, as described. Be sure to put the actions (jobs) from the risk analysis back into your plan.

CHAPTER 10

How Do We Keep the Show on the Road?

Once you've used your plan to decide exactly what you're going to do, you're ready to start your project. Then you need to make sure (a) that you follow what the plan says as closely as possible, and (b) that you are aware of, and respond to, the inevitable changes/unexpected things/firefights that occur along the way.

Your plan acts as your best guide and friend through the uncharted waters of the project. The plan tells you what should be happening on the project. You then need to ensure that what happens on the project gets reflected in the plan so that the two things stay synchronised. I hope you can now see that, first of all, the plan is a living document. It is constantly changing as the project unfolds. Furthermore the plan is always a simulation of the project, and so you can – at any time – try out the kind of 'what-if' scenarios we described in Chapter 8.

I'm also going to get you to record what actually happens ('the actuals') on your project. I hope you can see the value of doing this. To begin with, you start to get a sense very quickly of how accurate your plan was. If you find, for instance, that everything is taking twice as long as you had expected then this is nature's way of telling you that you should look again at your estimates – because if this trend carries through to the rest of the project then the whole thing is going to take much longer than your plan had predicted.

On the other hand, if the actuals are coming in very close to the estimates then this is greatly reassuring and increases your confidence, not just in your plan, but in the project generally. Also, if you religiously record what happens on your project then, on the day the project ends, your plan contains what actually happened. No estimates, no assumptions, rather the warts-and-all record of how the project actually unfolded. Imagine how valuable this information will be to you when you come to plan your next project. Even if your next project is very different from your current one, there will almost certainly be knowledge and information that can be carried over to your new plan. This, in turn, will increase the accuracy of the estimates in your next plan. Do this enough and you should become very good indeed at estimating.

It's also highly likely that your stakeholders will want to know how things are going. That being the case, you're going to have to give them some kind of status report.

In this chapter we talk about doing these things.

Tracking the project

Here's the easiest way I know to track your project. Do the following:

1. Take out your plan. What you see are lots and lots of jobs spread out over the timescale of the project. For example, look at the plan for this book again, opposite.
2. Now, in that timescale, find today. Today intersects some jobs but not others. To put it another way, some jobs require some action by you today, some don't.
3. Identify the ones that require some action by you today. This is your to-do list for this project.
4. Go and do these things, i.e. do what the plan says you're meant to do.
5. When a job finishes, record what actually happened. Your plan told you what was meant to happen. If it does that's great, you can record that fact. For example, you estimated a certain work and duration and budget for a job and, hey, that's what actually happened. Alternatively something different happened, i.e. some or all of the work/duration/budget weren't what you predicted. OK – so write down what actually happened. In the following example I show this for a little project called 'Write specification' consisting of three jobs – draft, review and update specification. (Because all the jobs occur in sequence, it's allowable on this occasion to add up the durations.) In this example there was slightly more work in the project than we had predicted (7 versus 6 person-days); but the project took 40 per cent longer than we had anticipated (14 days versus the 10 originally estimated).

FIGURE 10.1

The plan for writing this book

ID	Info	Task Name	Duration in days	Start	Finish	Prede	Resource
1		1. Get Your Life Back	85	3/6/08	29/9/08		
2		1.1. 60,000 words @1,000 words a day @ 3 days per week	85	3/6/08	29/9/08		
3	✓	1.1.1. 1-10,000 words	5	3/6/08	9/6/08		Fergus
4	✓	1.1.2. 10,000-15,000	11.5	10/6/08	25/6/08	3	Fergus
5	✓	1.1.3. 15,000-20,000	4.5	25/6/08	1/7/08	4	Fergus
6	✓	1.1.4. 20,000-30,000 @ 5,000 pw	19	2/7/08	28/7/08	5	Fergus
7	✓	1.1.5. 30,000-40,000	18	29/7/08	21/8/08	6	Fergus
8	✓	1.1.6. 40,000-50,000	8	22/8/08	2/9/08	7	
9	✓	1.1.7. One third to Headline	3	3/9/08	5/9/08	8	
10	✓	1.1.8. Two thirds to Headline	3	6/9/08	10/9/08		Fergus
11	✓	1.1.9. Parts 1-5 to Headline	3	11/9/08	15/9/08	10	
12	✓	1.1.10. Contingency	10	16/9/08	29/9/08	11	
13	✓	1.2 End	-	29/9/08	29/9/08	12	

JOB RECORD

	1 WRITE SPECIFICATION	1.1 DRAFT SPECIFICATION	1.2 REVIEW SPECIFICATION	1.3 UPDATE SPECIFICATION
Planned work (in person-days)	6	3	2	1
Planned duration (in days)	10	3	5	2
Planned budget (in £)	1,800	900	600	300
Actual work (in person-days)	7	4	2	1
Actual duration (in days)	14	4	5	5
Actual budget (in £)	2,100	1,200	600	300

6. Now see whether there was anything that happened on your project today that the plan hadn't predicted. In other words, were there any changes today? If not, that's great. If there were changes then you'll have to deal with them in one of the three ways that we talked about in Chapter 7, i.e.
   - Say it's a big change
   - Use contingency to cover the change
   - Suck it up – work more to deal with the change.

7. If the change is big then you must alter your plan and tell the stakeholders what the revised plan now is. If they accept this plan then this is what you now go forward with. If, on the other hand, they decide not to carry out this change, then you stay with the original plan.

8. If the change isn't big then you can either cover it using the contingency or you can work more hours/days to cover the change. The choice is up to you. However, I would generally advise being a bit miserly with your contingency in the early part of your project – you may need it later.

9. Finally, as a result of doing all of this, one of three things will happen to the project date (and the project budget, if you're tracking it and the total work in the project, if you're tracking that). I'll describe it for the date first. The date will either stay put, go right or go left. If the

date stays put, then you're on target – so far, your prediction has come true. If the date goes left then you're running ahead of schedule. That's nice. No need to do anything. If the date goes to the right then you're running behind schedule. One of these by itself isn't fatal, but if the *trend* is to the right, i.e. if every time you track the project the date moves further to the right, then it means that your project is drifting. In that case you're going to have to tell the bad news to the stakeholders and re-estimate the project. The same comments apply to the budget and the work. They either stay put, go up or go down. If they stay put then you're on target – so far, your prediction has come true. That's good. If they go down then you're ahead of budget and you haven't used all the person-days you had expected. That's nice. No need to do anything else. If they go up then you're running over budget and have used more person-days than you had predicted. One of these by itself isn't fatal, but if the *trend* is upwards, i.e. if every time you track the project the budget and work go up even more, then it means that your project is drifting. In that case you're going to have to tell the bad news to the stakeholders and re-estimate the project.

10. And that's it. The result is an updated plan which accurately reflects the status of the project on the ground.

Working ahead

Here's a variation of the basic tracking that I rather like. The only difference is that instead of looking at *today* on your timescale, you look at *this week*. You find anything that requires some action by you this week, put it on your to-do list and go and do it through the process as described above. Now you're working ahead, pushing your project forward as quickly and efficiently as possible.

How often should you track your project?

I'd say let the project be your guide. Maybe when you're starting out on the project, do the routine above every day. Then, once the project has settled down and you feel things are going pretty smoothly, you could maybe relax the discipline a bit and do it every two or three days. If, by doing that, you found you were starting to feel a little less in control and that some mistakes were occurring or there was some kind of drift (on the duration, the work or the budget) which you ought to have picked up on, then you could tighten up your tracking and go back to doing it more often. In the closing stages of the project, when you're literally running out of time, you might want to do it every day again. The choice is up to you. A short project that is critical to the organisation might need tracking every day. This would be overkill on a long project that isn't such a high priority. Take the basic routine as described above and make it work for you with the particular project.

Status reporting

Most status reporting that you see or hear is pretty worthless. Maybe you've seen the wonderful Dilbert cartoon where the office staff is at a meeting. The boss says, 'Let's go round the table and give an update on each of our projects.' Dilbert says, 'My project is a pathetic series of poorly planned, near-random acts. My life is a tragedy of emotional desperation.' The boss says, 'It's more or less customary to say that things are going fine.' Dilbert says, 'I think I need a hug.'

It's so profoundly true. It *is* more or less customary to say that 'things are going fine'. Generally people are unlikely to give out any kind of useful information about a project – and certainly not bad news – until they're really forced to.

In my experience, people don't do decent status reporting for one of the following reasons:

- Maybe they never had a plan in the first place
- Or they did but they never tracked progress against the plan
- Or they did but they didn't like what they saw
- Or they did, they didn't like what they saw and they're not going to tell anybody about it until they're really forced to.

I think most of us have seen and heard lousy status reporting. Here are some verbal examples:

Question: 'How's it going there, Charlie?'

Answer: 'Great' or 'It's all under control,' or the terrifying, 'We're 90 per cent done'. (Which generally means that 90 per cent of the time we allowed for the project has gone. It doesn't necessarily mean that 90 per cent of the thing has been done.)

And then we have the written ones. Perhaps you've seen them. They're full of stuff like, 'tasks completed last week', 'tasks planned for next week', 'critical issues', 'percentage complete', 'we did this', 'that thing happened' – to quote Shakespeare, 'full of sound and fury signifying nothing'.

So we've got to do decent status reporting. We've got to:

- Say how we're doing versus what we had predicted
- Say how we got to be where we are
- Allow stakeholders the option of looking at the plan for themselves.

Here – precisely – is how to do that. Whether it's written or verbal think of it as being in three 'layers' as follows:

Layer 1

How are we doing with regard to the date, the budget, the total work we'd estimated? Are we going to miss the date? Blow the budget? Did we underestimate the work? So you might say or write:

'No problem with regard to date, budget and work estimated.'

Or:

'On target to hit the date; budget may be a little bit over; work estimate was correct.'

Or:

'We're in trouble on this project and it looks like we're going to have to replan it.'

In addition, in this layer of the status report you want to say if you need help. Many things that occur on a project have to be sorted out by you. That's your job if you 'own' the project. But sometimes, other people – other stakeholders – may be the only people to sort out certain issues. You may need them to make a decision or provide you with some resources or remove a roadblock from the project. For example, in Green Cleaning Services, that decision to take a week out of your holidays may not be yours to make alone. You may require input from your significant other. So then, you might say (!):

'What would you think of me taking a week out of my holidays to get this thing off the ground?'

Or more generally, you might say or write:

'I need a decision on this particular issue.'

Or:

'Remember I need some of your department's people, Mr Stakeholder, in order to do the next piece of the project.'

So this is what the first layer of your status report reads or sounds like. It is one or two sentences that convey everything the stakeholders need to know about the overall status of the project.

Layer 2

How did we get to be where we are? Here you would record the major changes that occurred on the project during its life. And here it is almost certainly better to write them down – first, so that you don't forget and second, so your stakeholders don't.

So supposing in Green Cleaning Services you decided to start hunting for office business earlier – or even more dramatically – you decided to leave your day job so that you could pursue this full-time. You would record those major changes here – writing exactly what had happened. For example:

'On such and such a date decided not to hire foreperson but to quit and do the job myself.'

Or, more generally:

'On this date the stakeholders asked to have the project scope increased by adding in blah blah blah.'

Or:

'On this date lost two people to another project. Had to revise the delivery date of the project accordingly. The new delivery date is now...'

Layer 3

Finally, you can think of layer 3 as the everything-but-the-kitchen-sink layer. Here you don't have to write anything. You can just attach (or give) them copies of your plan in whatever form (Gantt Chart, spreadsheet or whatever) you think will be most useful to them.

So you can see there's not much writing here, not much work that you have to do, but it gets the picture across. Send this out once a week, as close to the end of the week as possible, and you're in business.

Assessing a project in five minutes

Here's one final thing that you may find useful in terms of keeping projects on the straight and narrow. It's how to assess a project in five minutes. If you've ever watched TV hospital dramas like *ER* you'll have heard the emergency room doctors talking about patients' 'vital signs'. Projects also have vital signs. There are a handful of things, the presence or absence of which indicates healthy or unhealthy projects respectively. If somebody is explaining the status of their project to you and you find your eyes glazing over as you're subjected to a relentless load of dreary data and charts, then here's how to cut through all of that to find out what's really happening.

You're going to measure and score the project against the following criteria:

ASSESSMENT	
CRITERION	**AVAILABLE SCORE**
1. How well defined or not is the goal?	20
2. Is there a final, definitive detailed list of jobs where every job has been broken down to the 1–5-day level of detail?	20
3. Does the project have somebody who, day-to-day, shepherds all of the jobs forward?	10
4. Are there people to do all of the jobs identified in 2? Do those people have enough time availability to devote to the project?	10
5. Is there contingency in the plan?	5
6. Has an up-to-date risk analysis been done and are the jobs to reduce those risks part of the project plan?	5
TOTAL	70

Doing the scoring

1. This is a measure of how well defined the goal is. The acid test here is that if you were to ask each stakeholder what the goal of the project is, and if each were to give you almost exactly the same reply, then the goal is well defined. Otherwise it is not. You only get a 20 when the project is complete because only then do you know exactly what was achieved. Pick a number between 0 and 20.

2. This is a measure of how complete the list of jobs is. Zero is no list. You might get 2 or 3 for a high-level breakdown, i.e. only the big pieces of the project. You only get 20 when the project completes because only then do you know exactly what the list of jobs was. Pick a number between 0 and 20. If the goal (Step 1) scores low, then this will score low because, if you won't know what you're trying to do, how could you have a list of jobs to do it?

3. If the leader can be named and that person has adequate time available to run the project, then give 10, otherwise give 0.

4. If there aren't any/enough people to do the work, score this 0 or low. Also take into account that this step should be in the same proportion as Step 2, e.g. a 14/20 for Step 2 would give at most a 7/10 for Step 4.

5. Allocate the 10 in two 5s. The first 5 is for contingency. The more contingency, the higher the score out of 5.

6. The second 5 is for how well or badly the risk-reducing activities have been identified and are being carried out.

Interpreting the scores

1. If the goal isn't right, nothing will be right

If the goal isn't right, you miss one of the two opportunities to get a high score, but notice how it all unravels now. If you don't know what you're trying to do, creating a list of jobs to do it is impossible. (So too, it's worth noting, is setting the expectations of the stakeholders. If you don't know what you're trying to do, how could you set them? What will happen then is that everyone will set his or her own expectations.) Thus the list is flawed resulting in missing the other opportunity to get a high score. If the list is flawed then shepherding the project forward (3) is impossible, as is assigning people to the jobs (4). Contingency (5) and risk analysis (6) will also have no meaning.

2. 40 is an important threshold

A project's vital sign score should start off low when the project is born and rise steadily over the life of the project. Initially projects may not score more than 40, and this can just mean that there is more work to be done in terms of scoping the project (1) and planning it (2 to 6). However, a project should quickly go above 40 and stay above it. (Notice that the latter isn't guaranteed, and a project can drop back again. This could happen, for example, if a major change to the scope of the project, went uncontrolled.)

3. Low scores always point you at the priority problem areas

Which is nice, I think you'll agree.

4. You can do anything you like on a poorly planned project and it won't make a blind bit of difference

You may have heard of Brooks' Law (see Frederick P. Brooks, *The Mythical Man Month* (1995)) – 'Adding people to a late project makes it later.' I believe that the above statement – 'you can do anything you like...' – can be viewed as a generalisation of Brooks' Law. It basically says that if your project gets into difficulties, go back and look at the plan; don't just, for example, blindly ask everyone to work harder. The problem is in the plan, not in the execution of the plan.

Example of scoring

The following is based on a real project. Suppose you were faced with the following problem. A project which is scheduled to take 17 months has been running for 11. There are about 250 people working on it. The project is very significant to the organisation and so a very senior person has been given the job of running it. There is lots of activity on the project. People are working long hours. Is the project in good shape or not?

Using your checklist above to guide you in your investigation, you uncover the status given in column three of the following table. You then score the project as described in column four.

CRITERION	AVAIL. SCORE	STATUS	ACTUAL SCORE
1. How well defined or not is the goal?	20	Specifications for much of the project still don't exist even though the project is due to end in 6 months.	Based on the proportion of specifications completed to those still not done, you score the project 14.
2. Is there a final, definitive detailed list of jobs where every job has been broken down to the 1–5-day level of detail?	20	Some parts of the project have plans, some parts have no plans. The bits that haven't been specified have no plans.	Since only 70 per cent (14/20) of the project is defined, this is the most that this could score. A 70 per cent would be possible if all of the bits of the project that were specified had plans. However, some don't. Score this 10.
3. Does the project have somebody who, day-to-day, shepherds all of the jobs forward?	10	The very senior person still has all their other responsi-bilities, so they don't give anywhere near enough time to devote to a project of this magnitude. In addition, they see the day-to-day shepher-ding of the project as work that is really beneath them.	This project doesn't have a leader. It has somebody with the title but nobody doing the job. Score 0.
4. Are there people to do all of the jobs identified in 2? Do those people have enough time avail-ability to devote to the project?	10	See 2.	Since only 50 per cent (10/20) of the jobs are identified, this could score no more than 50 per cent. Give it 5.
5. Is there contingency in the plan?	5	No.	Score 0.
6. Has an up-to-date risk analysis been done and are the jobs to reduce those risks part of the project plan?	5	No.	Score 0.
TOTAL	70		29

Conclusion? The project is two-thirds of the way through its planned life and yet its vital signs score is well below 40. The project is in disastrous shape and is going nowhere. It has no chance of succeeding in its current form and will seriously overshoot its budget and its deadline. To rescue this project, the following need to be done in the order indicated:

1. Replan the project. (By including contingency in the plan and doing a risk analysis, scores 5 and 6 will both climb.)

2. Use the plan to reset the expectations of the stakeholders. (This will not be a pleasant exercise.)
3. Complete the specifications. This will cause the 14/20 score to climb.
4. With the goal specified it will be possible to finalise the detailed list of jobs (causing the 10/20 to climb).
5. Now people will be working on the right things and everything else should start falling into place.

PART THREE: YOUR ORGANISATON

The third part of the book turns the focus on the organisation in which you work. Often people blame the organisation for which they work for being unable to work less and achieve more. They blame the culture of the organisation or its management or the sector in which the organisation operates. This part of the book shows you that while there may be truth in all of these things, there is usually a more fundamental issue in operation. Unsurprisingly, once again, this issue is supply and demand – this time viewed at an organisational level.

Chapter 11 shows you how to assess what might be happening in your organisation. If what's happening is a problem, Chapter 12 tells you how to fix it.

What's Wrong with the Organisation?

Why not let Fate run your organisation?

The place where I get work done on my car delivers what I would regard as outstanding customer service. By this I mean that any time they make a promise they keep it. If they say they'll have my car ready at a particular time, they do. If I've asked them to do a number of things to the car, I can be sure that they'll have done them – and they may even throw in a wash or valeting, if they have time. It's clear to me that they have their supply and demand sorted. When I call to make an appointment to get my car serviced, they find me a slot. Sometimes it's not the slot I want, but they'll explain why. 'We have so many cars that day,' they'll say, 'and a typical car takes so long, so that's why we can't do it today.' Supply and demand.

I have no idea what the guy who runs this smooth car maintenance operation earns. I'd be pretty sure though that it isn't as much as the typical CEO of even a small company. And as for the larger private or publicly quoted companies then I'm sure those CEOs earn many multiples of this man's salary. Which is strange because, in my opinion, this guy is probably doing a far better job for his boss than are the leaders of almost every company I've ever come across.

Let me explain.

Here's what happens in most companies. At the beginning of the year, the owners or shareholders decide that they want to grow business as usual by, say, 15 per cent. They also want to do some brand new things – new products, services, initiatives, take new directions. The management team takes this mission and launches lots of projects. Everybody in the organisation now has (a) maybe a day job and (b) almost certainly, a project-related workload. Most management teams expect everybody to undertake this workload. They say things like, 'That's just the culture here', or 'I don't want to hear anybody using the word "can't"', or 'We like a can-do attitude here', or 'Don't bring me problems, bring me solutions', or 'We're going to have to learn to do more with less', or – if somebody objects to all of this – 'You're being inflexible'.

If the management team is a bit more enlightened it will tell people to schedule themselves, say, 70 per cent for their day job and the remaining 30 per cent for project work. While this is a great idea in theory, it almost never happens on the ground. And anyway, how can somebody schedule themselves 70 per cent for their day job if it's a full-time job? Not do some bit of it? Which bit?

The troops begin to work harder and harder, longer and longer hours. Despite this the projects start to drift. Eventually there's a bit of a stink about some project. Some senior manager or it may be a customer begins to jump up and down about 'their' project. If they shout loud enough people are switched to that project and the project that lost the people is told to work harder. They do – but it doesn't make any difference. That project now starts to drift, despite the long hours being worked. And the project to which people were moved doesn't necessarily speed up. There are learning curves and people need to come up to speed and they make mistakes that people who were already on the project had thought were no longer being made.

Things carry on until another project is seen to be drifting. The same things happen – a stink, jumping up and down, people being moved from one project to another, the progress on more and more projects not being what was expected.

Eventually the end of the year comes round. Some projects have been done, some haven't. Many have come in late and/or over budget. Some people are burnt out and leave. Everybody thinks it was a tough year, but they worked really hard. There is a sense of having triumphed in the face of adversity. We definitely earned our salaries and bonuses this year.

But in fact, it could be argued that management wasn't really running the company at all. It was Fate that was running the company. It was Fate that decided what things got done and what things didn't. The particular combination of:

- Supply/demand imbalance
- People who shouted the loudest

• The sequence in which resources were swapped around determined
  what got done and what didn't.

Let's not forget too the additional overhead introduced by swapping
people around on projects – learning curves, time spent coming up to
speed or extra time needed when somebody returns to a project they
haven't worked on in a while. This overhead adds to the demand making
the supply/demand imbalance even worse than it had been at the
beginning of the year.

It would be as though my garage drew lots to see which cars they would
work on in a particular week. And from time to time they would stop work
on a particular car and then return to it some time later. And they would
work very long hours while doing all of this. It'd be mad, wouldn't it?

Stretch goals

A lot of bosses or organisations these days like to talk about 'stretch goals'
or 'ambitious targets' or 'aggressive schedules' or 'tough challenges'.

I have no problem with any of this. Organisations *should* stretch. Our
reach should exceed our grasp. But there's a difference between stretch
goals and losing the plot. And too many organisations, in my experience,
lose the plot.

We talked in Chapter 3 about supply and demand. There we applied it to
a person. But the concept of supply and demand can also be applied to
organisations. And organisations lose the plot when they either forget
about supply and demand or are never conscious of it in the first place. Let
me illustrate.

A few years ago a technology company of about a hundred people called
us up and asked if we would do some project management training for
them. I went to meet the CEO – to try to understand the problems they
were trying to solve. 'There are essentially two sides to the business,' he
explained, 'Sales & Marketing and Product Delivery. Sales & Marketing keep
complaining that Product Delivery never hit any of their deadlines, never
deliver anything on time and – basically – can't be believed when they
make commitments. Product Delivery keeps complaining that Sales &
Marketing are always giving them impossible deadlines and keep changing

their minds about what exactly they want. Everybody is working incredibly long hours and we believe this is a project management problem. If Product Delivery could run their projects using best-practice project management, then all these problems should go away, or, at least, be significantly reduced.'

I said we would be happy to do the training but we'd like to do another piece of work first. What we did was this. We got the management team together and, looking forward eighteen months, we:

- Listed all the projects they were currently doing
- Added to the list all the additional projects they planned to do during this period
- Made some assumptions about new projects that might come in from customers during this time
- Added in business-as usual-things like support for existing products and customers, training, dealing with new customer requests and so on.

We then estimated how much work would go into each of these over this period. We added all these up and came out with (in round numbers) 6,000 person-weeks' worth of work. We then listed all the people that were currently in the organisation plus the number that they were planning to hire over the eighteen-month period. We calculated how much work each of these would contribute over that period. The number came out at 2,000 person-weeks.

I still remember the moment when I was summarising all of this for the management team and, in particular, the CEO. I wrote the two numbers on a flipchart and then said, 'So, you have two options. You can cut the number of projects by two-thirds or you can hire three times as many people.' I stopped speaking and there was a silence for, it seemed like, twenty or thirty seconds. I think they were waiting for me to say, 'Or you could do this or you could do that.' When they realised I had finished, somebody said, 'What about increasing efficiency?' Sure, that might get them 15 or 20 per cent more capacity (supply). But if the basic problem is that demand exceeds supply by a factor of three, then efficiency isn't going to fix that problem. Looking for efficiencies will be just like rearranging the deck chairs on the *Titanic*.

Just to finish off the story, there followed a period of denial and head-shaking and there-must-be-another way. When they realised there wasn't, when they realised how implacable supply and demand are, they did a combination of the two things I had mentioned. They planned to hire a few more people but mainly they had to cut the list. They had to go back to customers and change delivery dates, renegotiate contracts, drop products. It was an incredibly painful experience. But the eventual result was that that they took back control of their business from Fate.

x and 3x

In our company, this scenario of a company's demand exceeding its supply is now known as the 'x and 3x' problem (x being the 2,000 person-weeks and 3x being the 6,000). The story I've described is the most extreme example of this I've ever seen. However, I've done this exercise many times since and I've almost always found it to be true that the organisation's demand exceeds its supply. I've seen x and 1.3x, x and 1.5x, x and 2x. If this is your organisation then you need to do something about it. Irrespective of the size and scale of your organisation you need to know its supply and demand, and you need to cut the demand to match the supply. Only then can you be sure that the things you are trying to do will get done.

If you're running such an organisation you need to calculate its supply and demand. And if you work in such an organisation, and feel that you're powerless, a victim, then – you're not. Do this calculation yourself and then bring it to the attention of your boss. It would probably ruin his whole day, but it'd be the first step in tackling the problem.

Why do organisations do this?

As it's described above, the x and 3x behaviour – if I can refer to it as that – is not very sensible. It results in waste (of time, resources and money), missed deadlines, overspends, nasty surprises, stress, missed opportunities and lack of work/life balance. So why is it that so many organisations do it?

You may remember in Chapter 4 I quoted from Tom DeMarco's book, *The Deadline*. Here's one of the things it says: 'Perhaps managers make so much use of pressure because they don't know what else to do, or are daunted by how difficult the alternatives are.' I think that within this sentence are some hints that may help us answer the question.

First of all I think organisations and bosses do this because they've always done this. They don't know another way and can't envisage that there might be another way. Also, because everybody ends up working so hard, there's a feeling that it has to be the right way because it is so hard. No pain no gain.

Because organisations/bosses feel there is no other way then they are afraid of trying anything else. There is an assumption that nothing else can/will work. The fact that an alternative might be based around a terribly simple idea – supply and demand – makes it even more, not less, scary. We're all dead smart people, they reckon – we couldn't possibly have missed something so elementary. And the notion that we could run a successful organisation where we didn't work all the hours God sends, seems absolutely too terrifying to contemplate. My goodness – if we did that, our superiors would feel we weren't committed. Or worse still they would ask what could we achieve if we went back to working long hours.

It all adds up to a potent – but completely delusional – mix.

What would it be like if organisations didn't do this?

The answer is that it would actually be pretty nice. We would decide at the beginning of the year what we could and couldn't do. We would assign our resources, they would work regular hours and routinely deliver what they predicted. There would a lot less firefighting and fewer nasty surprises. There would be a lot less job-related stress. There would be very little additional overhead caused by flipping resources from one thing to another. The company would make more money because it would always deliver on its commitments and there would be reduced waste of time, money, resources and energy.

You may be saying that this sounds like fantasyland, the happiest kingdom of them all. I'll say it's nothing of the sort. I know companies that run like this – not many, admittedly, but some. If you would like to join this small group of companies, the next chapter shows you how.

CHAPTER 12

Taking Back Your Organisation from Fate

It is possible to take back your organisation from Fate and this chapter gives you the mechanics of doing exactly that. If you run such an organisation I believe you have no choice but to do it. And if you work in such an organisation then I think it's not enough to just consider yourself a victim in all this. I think it behoves you to come up with the facts and show them to the powers that be. In either case, here's what you must do.

I should also mention – indeed you may have already thought of it – that getting things done is not just a question of numbers of people. It is also a question of skill, knowledge, experience, expertise, motivation. Quite right. But I hope you can see that until you sort out the supply and demand question, then the issue of people's knowledge and expertise is a bit irrelevant. If you don't have enough people to do the work then all the knowledge and experience in the world isn't going to make a difference.

1. Decide the timeframe/planning horizon you want to look at

You can pick any timeframe you like, but here's what I'd recommend. Take what remains of this year, for example. Or if you're at that point in the year where you're beginning to plan for next year, then take from now to the end of next year.

2. Measure the organisation-wide demand

1. Make a list of all the projects that your organisation is definitely going to do in the period. This, on its own, can be a useful exercise. Often,

while doing it, you hear people saying, 'Hey, I didn't know we were doing that project', or 'I thought that project was over', or 'Who approved that project?'

2. There will be other projects that are perhaps, dependent on winning contracts or orders. For these you will have to make some assumptions as to which ones you are likely to get and which you will not. Make what seem like the most realistic assumptions you can.

3. Add to your list any other business-as-usual type stuff.

4. This table contains an example of what such a list might look like:

LIST OF PROJECTS

KNOWN PROJECTS

Project A
Project B
Norway version
Holland version
Denmark version
Project C
Project D
Norway version
Holland version
Denmark version
Project E
Norway version
Holland version
Denmark version
Project F
Norway version
Holland version
Denmark version
Project G
Norway version
Holland version
Denmark version
Project H
Project I
Variant 1
Variant 2

NEW PROJECTS – ASSUMED

Project J
Project K
Project L
Project M
Project N
Project O

BUSINESS AS USUAL

Support of existing products and systems
Researching new technologies
Training
Contingency

5. Now you need to figure out how much work is involved in each of these things over the given period. Here's how to do that.

Ideally, each project has a plan which has been estimated as we described in Chapter 8. If that's the case then just take the figure for the total work (not the duration) in that project and add it to a second column. Hopefully some of your projects will have plans and it will be just a case of lifting the figures.

For those projects that don't have plans you have a few possibilities. The first (and most accurate) is to estimate the total work in each project as described in Chapter 8. The second possibility – it will be less accurate but give you an answer quicker – is to break each project down into its big chunks of work. (Again refer to Chapter 8.) Then, having done that, try to estimate (essentially guess) the amount of work in each of these chunks. A third possibility – probably less accurate again, but again quicker – would be to classify the projects into some classification scheme such as Small, Medium, Large, Extra Large. Then, once again, you would try to estimate (guess!) the size of each of these four classifications. For example, you might say that a Small project was about 5 person-months, a Medium one 10 person-months, a Large one 20 person-months and an Extra Large was 50 person-months.

However you choose to do it, here's what your list might look like then:

LIST OF PROJECTS WITH TOTAL WORK SHOWN (DEMAND)

KNOWN PROJECTS	TOTAL WORK IN THAT PROJECT (in person-weeks)
Project A	**.8**
Project B	**.541**
Norway version	*.305*
Holland version	*.172*
Denmark version	*.64*
Project C	**.48**
Project D	**.440**
Norway version	*.312*
Holland version	*.64*
Denmark version	*.64*
Project E	**.368**
Norway version	*.232*
Holland version	*.68*
Denmark version	*.68*
Project F	**.134**
Norway version	*.94*
Holland version	*.20*
Denmark version	*.20*
Project G	**.976**
Holland version	*.720*
Norway version	*.128*
Denmark version	*.128*
Project H	**.1,032**
Project I	**.32**
Variant 1	*.800*
Variant 2	*.100*
NEW PROJECTS – ASSUMED	**.100**
Project J	**.256**
Project K	**.128**
Project L	**.128**
Project M	**.392**
Project N	**.152**
Project O	**.240**
BUSINESS AS USUAL	**.176**
Support of existing products and systems	**.988**
Researching new technologies	**.96**
Training	**.40**
Contingency	**.50**
TOTAL	**.9,684 person-weeks**

3. Measure the organisation-wide supply

1. List all of the people existing or to be hired in the period and who will contribute work towards the projects.
2. Figure out how much work they will contribute. The table below shows an example of this kind of calculation:

CALCULATION OF SUPPLY

	START	END	NUMBER OF MONTHS	NUMBER OF STAFF	TOTAL PERSON-MONTHS*
Existing staff	1/7/08	31/12/08	18	19	342
New hires	1/1/09	31/12/09	12	6	72
				TOTAL	414
			TOTAL (in person-weeks) i.e. total in person-months multiplied by 4		1,656

There are 19 people currently. Over the period under investigation (18 months), this gives 342 (18 X 19) person-months effort from current staff. 6 new staff are to be hired from January 2009. This will add an extra 72 (12 X 6) person-months to supply. Adding these two figures together provides a total of 414 person-months' worth of effort. This is equivalent to 1,844 weeks (using 4.2 person-weeks = 1 person-month).

*Column 4 multiplied by column 5

4. Make the cut/prioritise the list

At this point there are a few possibilities. One is that supply is greater than or equal to demand. In other words, you have more than enough people to do all the work. That's great. Now you can start making sure you have the right skills and knowledge available.

However, if the opposite is true, if demand exceeds supply, then you have a problem. You are trying to do too much with too little and it's not going to work. This means that you're going to have to prioritise your list and decide what gets done and what doesn't. Will this be a happy experience? Probably not. But it's got to be done if you're to take your organisation back from Fate. How do you do it? Well, you've already seen prioritisation. You did it earlier for your own projects. It's exactly the same for the organisation's projects. Let's do it.

You say, 'If I could only do one project on this list, what would it be?' That becomes your number-one priority. Then you take the remaining list and say, 'If I could only do one project on this list, what would it be?' That becomes your number-two priority. You continue doing this until the list is prioritised. Then you cut the list where supply equals demand. It's vicious prioritisation – only this time for the organisation's projects.

This may take you a bit of time and it may take you several shots at it. What will emerge too, as you do it, will be what might grandly be called your 'prioritisation algorithm'. Or to put it more simply, how do you decide that one project is more important than another. What are the factors that determine that one project takes precedence over another? They could be all sorts of things – the project's budget, the number of people affected by it, the amount of savings or profits the project will contribute to the organisation, which customer the project is for and so on. When you've figured out what your prioritisation algorithm is, write it down. You're going to need it again in the future.

An example of a prioritisation algorithm – and note that it is just an example – might be that you say:

- The project budget is the most important factor, i.e. the bigger the budget, the more important the project;
- After that it's the customer for whom we're doing the project is the most important, i.e. if two projects have roughly similar budgets, we will give priority to that of customer A over customer B;
- And finally, we might say that within each customer we will give priority to projects that involve our organisation's new technology rather than old technology.

5. Manage the project priority list

Your organisation doesn't stay static. Projects complete, new projects or opportunities emerge, people come and go, the business environment changes. Thus, the exercise of prioritising the projects and matching supply to demand isn't a one-off thing. It needs to be done on a regular basis. Usually, when organisations first begin to do this, they find that they are updating the list very often – weekly or even twice a week, but quickly it settles down so that something more like once a fortnight or once a month should become the norm.

Prior to doing this exercise it may also have been the case that projects were constantly being born or used to pop up in a completely uncontrolled sort of way. For example, the boss or someone else higher up would suddenly announce that this new thing was now 'the number-one priority'. All of that should stop now. The random and uncontrolled birth of projects gets replaced by the following.

A process is put in place. (You'll sometimes hear it grandly described as a 'resource management process'.) It is a controlled way of deciding which projects the organisation is going to do and who's going to work on those projects. The process should work like this:

1. Anyone who has an idea for a project – no matter how important they are in the organisation – 'fills out the form', i.e. some kind of project request or project suggestion form.
2. The forms go into a hopper or in-tray.
3. Periodically – you can start with once a week, if you like – the group of people who decide about where resources should go, meet. The projects in the hopper are prioritised (using the prioritisation algorithm from earlier) and merged with the project list. Then you make the cut again, i.e. you cut the list once more where supply equals demand. Resources are moved around as necessary and if required.

One of the main things that will happen if you do this will be that the amount of chopping and changing that goes on will reduce enormously. Management become much more aware of the overhead involved in shunting people around. Because priorities have been decided explicitly there will be far fewer changes to priorities. All this stability should mean that more gets done with less firefighting, stress, waste and mistakes.

6. Report on the projects

Finally, you will want to report on the projects and here's a way you could do that. Figure 12.4 shows a general-purpose template that you could use as is. You could also use it as the basis for building your own – for example, if the people you were reporting to had other, specific requirements.

FIGURE 12.4

Status of projects: 14 January 2004

| # | PROJECTS | OWNER | DUE | BUDGET | | | DAYS | |
				Original	Used	Remaining	Original	Used
1			Dec-04					
2			Dec-04					
3			Dec-04					
4			Dec-04					
5			Dec-04					
6			Dec-04					
7			Nov-04					
8			Feb-04					
9			Feb-04					
10			Feb-04					
11			Nov-04					
12			Nov-04					
13			Dec-04					
14			Apr-04					
15			?					
16			Feb-04					
17			Dec-04					
18			Dec-04					
19			May-04					
20			Apr-04					
21			Sep-04					
22			?					
23								
24								
25			Apr-04					
26			Jan-05					
27			Aug-04					
28			Aug-04					
29			Aug-04					
30			Aug-04					

5 = Green = On track:
3 = Amber = Some problems but we're fixing them:
0 = Blue = No written plan exists:
-1 = Red = Runaway project:
Score is blank = White = Status unknown:

TOTAL NUMBER OF PROJECTS
The readabaility of this report can be greatly enhanced using the colour coding noted above. This is so-called 'traffic light' or 'RAG' [Red - Amber - Green] reporting, which is familiar to many people.

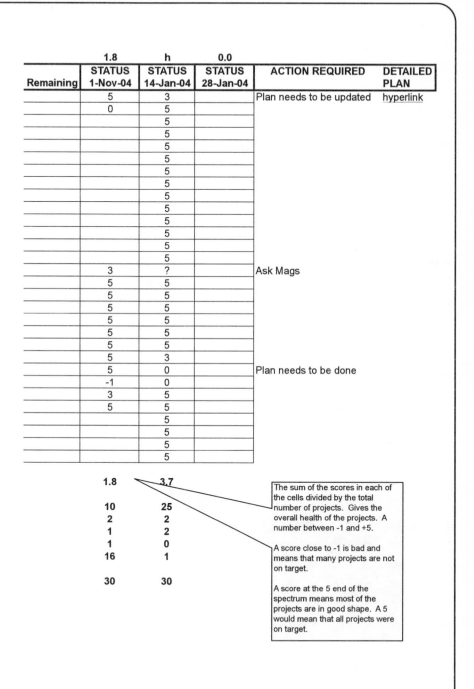

	1.8	h	0.0		
Remaining	STATUS 1-Nov-04	STATUS 14-Jan-04	STATUS 28-Jan-04	ACTION REQUIRED	DETAILED PLAN
	5	3		Plan needs to be updated	hyperlink
	0	5			
		5			
		5			
		5			
		5			
		5			
		5			
		5			
		5			
		5			
		5			
		5			
		5			
	3	?		Ask Mags	
	5	5			
	5	5			
	5	5			
	5	5			
	5	5			
	5	5			
	5	3			
	5	0		Plan needs to be done	
	-1	0			
	3	5			
	5	5			
		5			
		5			
		5			
		5			

1.8	3.7
10	25
2	2
1	2
1	0
16	1
30	30

The sum of the scores in each of the cells divided by the total number of projects. Gives the overall health of the projects. A number between -1 and +5.

A score close to -1 is bad and means that many projects are not on target.

A score at the 5 end of the spectrum means most of the projects are in good shape. A 5 would mean that all projects were on target.

Since the report is pretty busy, let me describe it for you. There are headings for:

- Project number
- Project name
- Project Manager (or Owner)
- The date the project is due
- The budget (planned, actually spent and remaining)
- Days used on the project (planned, actual and remaining)
- The status as it was on each of three successive dates. A further column would be added every time you reported on the status
- Any action required
- A hyperlink pointing to the detailed plan for this project.

In terms of the project status you could use colour coding or numbers (as I have done) to indicate the following status. You can also use both.

Green/5/On track i.e. plan exists and we're running to the plan;

Amber/3/Plan exists; we've drifted a bit but we're taking action to get it back on track;

Red/-1/Whether a plan exists or not, the project is out of control and needs to be replanned;

Blue/0/No written plan exists.

You may ask why use numbers rather than colours to indicate the status since, for most people, colours are a lot more visible and intuitive. The answer is that while that's definitely true, numbers give us a way of recording the overall status of the organisation's projects, i.e. they give us a way to 'add up the colours'. Think of it as describing the health of the organisation in terms of the health of its projects. If you assign numbers as shown in the status report, you can total them up, divide by the total number of projects and you will get a total number that ranges from -1 to 5. The closer that total is to 5 the better the health of all of your projects is. The closer it is to -1, the worse the state is. A -1 would mean that all your projects are out of control; a 5 would mean they're all on target. You could report this and publish this every week.

It's fair to say that if you haven't done this before then people become very edgy about the prospect of you doing it. So if you like the idea and would like to do it, but are worried about how people will react, here's a good way to start that's gentle and doesn't scare people. The first week you take the status to what you can think of as a 'soft audit'. A soft audit is nothing more than asking people the status of their project and taking their word for it, whatever they say. Here is a little template or form that you can use to do a soft audit on a project and to calculate the overall health of all the projects.

Soft audit: step-by-step instructions

SOFT AUDIT FORM

Q1.
Does the project have a plan?   Yes   No
                                                           (circle one)
Yes – go to Q2.
No – STOP – apply colour code blue and give the project a score of 0.
Record this score below.

Q2.
Is the project on target?   Yes   No
                                                           (circle one)
Yes – STOP – apply colour code green and give the project a score of
5. Record this score below.
No – go to Q3.

Q3.
How much is the project off target?   A little   A lot
                                                           (circle one)
A little – STOP – apply colour code amber and give the project a score
of 3. Record this score below.
A lot – go to Q4.

Q3.
Is the project out of control?   Yes   No
                                                           (circle one)
Yes – STOP – apply colour code red and give the project a score of -1.
Record this score below.
No – apply colour code amber and give the project a score of 3.

The project score   _____

ORGANISATION PERFORMANCE INDICATOR (OPI)

Instructions:
Take the soft audit score for each project and transfer the scores to this sheet, add up the total and divide by the number of projects. This is the OPI score.

Project Name	Score
1	
2	
3	
4	
5	
6	
7	
8	
9	
10	
11	
12	
13	
14	
15	
16	
17	
18	
19	
20	
21	
22	
23	
24	
25	

Total score ....

OPI score ....

The idea is that the first time you do this you do a soft audit and record that status in that column of your status report. Then the following – say – week, when you want to take a status you now start to check the veracity of the soft audits. So:

- If somebody reported that their project was Green (On target) then where's the (written) plan? Often Greens (On targets) turn out to be anything but.
- Often, too, Ambers (Off target a little bit) turn out to be Reds (Out of control and need to be replanned).

Conclusion

All of this may seem a long way from you trying to work less and achieve more. On the face of it, it may sound like lots of *extra* work, rather than less work. Yes, for sure, it's some extra work that you don't do at the moment, but the payback is enormous. If you run an organisation – a department, a section, a group, a division, a company – to do what I have described in this chapter will have some enormous benefits for you and the people for whom you work. These benefits include:

The ability to meet more of your commitments on time and within budget, resulting in:

- Happier 'customers' (i.e. the people for whom you work);
- Less wasted effort due to switching people from one project to another;
- Less crises and firefighting;
- Less stress and late nights for you and your organisation;
- A far clearer view of how your organisation is managing projects and where the weak points are.

PART FOUR:
YOUR LIFE

Work Less, Achieve More can also be applied to your life. It is possible to reshape or change your life using the three simple ideas we have spoken about:
- Learn to say 'no' nicely
- Learn to prioritise viciously
- A little planning is better than a lot of firefighting. How to do that is the subject of this part of the book.

There are three chapters. Chapter 13 goes over some essentials. Chapter 14 tells you how to identify the life you want – assuming, that is, that you don't already know. Chapter 15 tells you how to get the life you want.

CHAPTER 13

Essentials

What you need to do

It's really strange how in the time I have been writing this book I have come across so many people who are doing what they want to do and living the life they want to lead. In the last week alone – and this is not any kind of exaggeration – I have found the following:

- I met up with a friend of mine. We hadn't had any kind of a serious chat in about four years. During that time she had spent some time working for her company in San Francisco. During that same period, her husband gave up his job to go with her and, while there, he trained as an artisan baker. They are now back home, he has built his own wood-fired oven and is ready to start his bakery business. She has a more senior job than when she moved to the United States but she spends one day a week working from home. She also goes in late in the morning so that she can spend time with her children and avoid the traffic. Her children don't go to crèches because, between herself and her husband, they can take care of them.
- The person who is the subject of Case Study No. 1 (see Chapter 16).
- Another friend of mine, this one I hadn't seen for 15 years. During that time her husband gave up his job to become an acupuncturist and she works on average three days a week as a business consultant. They are very happy that they get to spend lots of time with their one child.
- Just yesterday I had an email from yet another long lost friend of mine who is moving house. She and her partner are moving from Canada to Virginia, USA. Nothing too extraordinary about that except that her email says that they are leaving now (July) but don't expect to be in Charlottesville until 'the end of the year'. Clearly they are planning to make an adventure out of it!

And that was just last week. I have to admit that last week was a particularly rich week for this kind of thing but that's not the point. The point is that you can change your life. Lots of so-called 'ordinary people' do it. If you're not happy with the life you're living, you can change it to be the one you want to live. The three little ideas that we have spoken about will enable you to do that. All it needs – once again – is the wish from you to want to change something and the will to stay at it until it happens.

You're going to be dead a long time. In the meantime, there's now – today, this week, this year, this life. If you're not happy with how your day/week/year/life is going then stop moaning about it, stop being stressed or unhappy – change it! And if you don't change it you've nobody to blame but yourself – not your family circumstances or background; not your financial circumstances; not your job or organisation or sector that you find yourself in; not the culture within which you work, not other people. Nothing. Nobody. Only yourself. If you went to the trouble and expense of buying this book then get some value out of it. If you don't already have one there's a great life out there waiting for you.

Go and find it!

How you're going to do it

Now maybe you already know what kind of life you want and if so, that's great. If not, how are you going to find out, how are you going to decide?

The question, 'What is the purpose of life?' has occupied philosophers for millennia. A lot of people constantly wonder about the purpose of their own lives. They are unhappy, restless and seem to think that 'if only' something were different – more money, more free time, a lottery win – things would be different. It's When-Then Syndrome: When this happens then I'll be happy. There are all sorts of methods, tests, books and people available that offer to help you to figure out what you want to do with your life. So you could go off down one of these roads. (In this regard you could do a lot worse than buying Richard Bolles Nelson's book *What Colour Is Your Parachute?* (2007).)

However, have you ever read that feature in the *Sunday Times* entitled 'A Life in the Day'? It's generally the last article in the colour magazine. In it, well-known (and sometimes not so well-known) people describe a typical day in their life. I've always been intrigued by it. I'm always intrigued by any insight into how people I admire spend their time.

As I may have mentioned earlier, what I really want to do is to earn my living from writing fiction. Thus, I'm always interested in how novelists spend their time. One of the writers I really like is Alan Furst and I read this about him recently. 'He spends mornings mapping the intricate world of his novels on yellow Post-it notes and pasting them meticulously into a frayed loose-leaf binder and afternoons digging in his wife's garden.' And looking on the author's website there is a section called 'Author Tour – 2008' listing the cities and bookstores he will be visiting in June 2008. If you want to know what a novelist's life is like then here is one example.

It has always seemed to me that how somebody wants to spend their days and weeks is as good a way as any other of figuring out what they want to do with their life. Sure, you should have goals – dreams of what you want to be or to do or to happen – but these need to relate to what you are going to do every day, every week, every month, every year. There are two reasons for this or more precisely, there are two benefits to thinking this way.

The first is that these things enable you to figure out what it is you really want to do. This is because imagining how you're going to spend your time – what life could be like if you could spend your days in a certain way – is surely the best guide to what you want your life to be like. Second, by starting to spend your time as you have imagined it, you can start to move towards the goals and objectives you want. This is what we are going to do in the next two chapters. In Chapter 14 I will get you to imagine how you would like to be spending your time. Then in Chapter 15 we will talk about how you can start to transition from where you are now to where you would like to be.

CHAPTER 14

Imagining the Life You Want

In Chapter 2 I talked about you having a list and I got you to make yours. This is my list as it is now. This list is the big picture of what I want to do. If you haven't done yours then now would be a good time to do it. If you've done one already, make sure it's up to date.

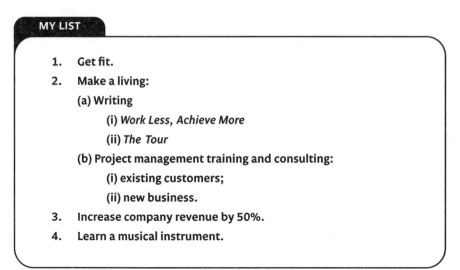

MY LIST

1. **Get fit.**
2. **Make a living:**
    (a) Writing
    　　　(i) *Work Less, Achieve More*
    　　　(ii) *The Tour*
    (b) Project management training and consulting:
    　　　(i) existing customers;
    　　　(ii) new business.
3. **Increase company revenue by 50%.**
4. **Learn a musical instrument.**

In Chapter 2 I also talked about having a daily list. This is mine:
1. 1 hour's writing
2. *On Becoming A Novelist*
3. ETP
4. 2,000 words
5. Exercise
6. Music

This is the list of how I would like to spend my day. This is my equivalent of 'A Life in the Day' or Alan Furst's Post-it notes in the morning and digging in his wife's garden in the afternoon. It is also my permanent list of 'A' items. Sometimes other things get added to it, sometimes not. Here's what the six things mean:

1. **1 hour's writing**: I like to do an hour's writing first thing when I wake up, while I'm still almost half asleep. The subconscious, which has been the source of dreams during the night, doesn't quite seem to have gone off-duty and sometimes good ideas pop up or I get a strong (and sometimes, unstoppable) flow of writing.

2. *On Becoming A Novelist*: The greatest book ever written for would-be novelists is John Gardener's *On Becoming A Novelist* (in my humble opinion). Whether I'm writing fiction or non-fiction, having done my hour, I like to read a page or two of it. It constantly reminds me of what's important in writing – any kind of writing.

3. **ETP**: After this I usually do the stuff that relates to my 'day job'. ETP is my company that does project management training and consulting. There'll usually be emails to answer, calls to make, proposals to write, that sort of thing.

4. **2,000 words**: After this, I'll try and take the morning writing, the one hour and add to it. I like to reach a daily target of at least 2,000 words. If I hit a good 'flow' then I could do better than that. Some days it's a struggle to make the 2,000.

5. **Exercise**: If I haven't done it already during the day, I will do it now.

6. **Music**: In the time I have been completing this book, I have started to get this off the ground. You may remember that in Chapter 2 I made this goal SMART – Specific, Measurable, Achievable, Realistic, Time-bound. I did this by deciding that I would choose what instrument I wanted to learn before the end of the year. Well, I've actually made lots of progress on this. I've decided I want to learn the guitar. Once that decision was made, a small royalty cheque happened to pop in the letterbox. And now the guitar is bought and is on its way to me. I have a book on how to learn to play and so the next target is to work my way through the book. So I'll have to find the time to do that during my day.

Once I've worked my way through items 1 to 4 then I regard my working day as over. This could be mid-morning, around lunch time or mid- to late afternoon. Whatever it is, at that point I stop and go do other things – cooking, go to the shops, having fun (not that work wasn't) or whatever. Once I've done items 5 and 6 I'll have done all the things I wanted to do that day.

All of this is my working day when I work from home – which happens to be in France. However, my day job – ETP – demands that I also spend time on the road. When I'm on the road, I try to follow my daily list as much as I can. Thus, I always try to do an hour's writing, I try to stay up to date with emails and ETP-related paperwork, I try to find time and space to exercise. Thus, I try to continue the routine that I like even when events conspire against it.

What I eventually want to do is get to the point where I do very little ETP stuff and that most of my time is devoted to novel writing. Then, I could probably spend more time working from home and less time on the road, which I also would prefer.

Why am I telling you all this?

I repeat once again: it's not because I want to bore you with the details of my life or that you need to know the minutiae of it. The routine that I've described may sound very dull to you, but that's OK – it's what I like to do. The reason I'm telling you this is that my routine describes my life and conversely, the life I want is determined by my routine and the way I spend my days.

So – if you want to identify the life you want, this is a good – and for me, the best and only – place to start. Write down – in as much detail as you can – how you would like things to be. Start with a day. In the life you want, what would a typical day be like? Where would you be living? With whom? What time would you get up? What would you do first? And then? Would you have a commute to do or would you be working from where you live? (Notice that even if in the life you want you will be as rich as Croesus and laze around all day you'll still have to have some kind of routine, so you should be able to write it down.) Where would you be working? What would you be doing? Who would you be working with? What role would you have? What type of things would fill your day? When would you finish? How would you know when you'd done enough work? What would you do then? How would you spend a typical evening? With whom? What time would you go to bed?

Now, if that was a typical day, what would a typical week be like? Would every day be a day like that or would there be different types? Would you look forward to Mondays – or at least, not mind them? Would you be sorry to finish work on a Friday because you'd like it so much? Would this become a problem? How would you spend the weekend? Write out the weekend days the same as you did the weekdays. Would you have more leisure time or 'quality time' (with children or family or friends, say) than you do at the moment?

And how would one month vary from the next? Would certain times of the year – summers, for example, be different from other times? Busier? Quieter? What would Christmas or Easter or any other traditional holiday periods be like? Would you be taking more holidays than you take now?

Are there people who are doing what you'd like to be doing? If so, what is a typical day/week/month/year in their life like? Get it all down in as much detail as you can.

And while you're at it, here's another thing that you could usefully do. Make a list of all of the people who are affected by your life at the moment – wives, husbands, partners, girlfriends, boyfriends, children, brothers, sisters, friends, work colleagues, bosses, customers and so on. Throw the net as wide as you can. Try not to miss anybody. Feel free to include the family pet, if you want. Be sure – and this is really important – to put yourself in the list.

Now, draw two columns to the right of the names. In the first column, write down for each of these people, whether they're happy or not with your life as it is at the moment. Next, in the second column write down how they would feel if you moved to your new life. A couple of possible things could happen if you do this exercise. The first is that more people would be happy if you moved to your new life. That's nice if that happens – it's extra incentive, if you needed it, to go for it.

But it may also happen that fewer people will be happy but that you will be far happier. Now you're in trouble – because now you're looking down the barrel of major guilt. You want to do something which many other people are not going to be happy with. It may be that your wife or husband or partner isn't going to be happy with the risk of you starting your own business. Or other people don't approve of somebody you have hooked up with. Or that you're going to make a move somewhere else, leaving people behind you. Or your work colleagues are going to disapprove of some action you're going to take. I'm not saying that you will deliberately set out to hurt people but it may well be that, as a result of the actions you are proposing to take, people will feel hurt – maybe significantly so.

What are you going to do in this situation?

It comes back to our basic proposition – that you only have one life/that life is a performance/that you're going to be dead a long time. In my opinion you've gotta do what you've gotta do – and that being the case, you've got to figure out a way to deal with the guilt. You could do nothing better than going out and spending a few pounds on *Your Erroneous Zones* by Wayne Dyer. Go to Chapter 5 and start reading. The chapter heading and the opening words say it all:

> **5 The Useless Emotions – Guilt and Worry**
> *If you believe that feeling bad or worrying long enough will change a past or future event, then you are residing on another planet with a different reality system. Throughout life, the two most futile emotions are guilt for what has been done and worry about what might be done.*

And so he goes on. He shows how guilt can completely immobilise you and stop you from taking any action. He explains how guilt is different from learning from the past. He describes the origins and sources of guilt and, best of all, he gives you some ideas for eliminating guilt. If all of that's a bit too Californian for you then you can do all of this yourself. You just need to work on it and do something about it.

I guess up until the time I began to do something about it, I had accumulated as much guilt as the next man. But then I started to work on it and in the intervening years I've managed to get rid of most of it. A couple of light bulbs have gone on.

- I can't change the past. No matter how much time and energy I put into it, I can't change the tiniest piece of it.
- I can't please all of the people all of the time. There will always be stuff about me that people are unhappy about. Even it's something tiny like

some mannerism or turn of speech, there will always be something. That being the case, all I can do is live my own life, try to love the people I care about – notice that this includes myself – and try not to hurt the people around me.

All of these are clichés I know – old sayings, hoary old chestnuts, statements of the bleedin' obvious – but there are deep truths in them. Ultimately, no matter how you do it, you've got to work it out for yourself. The light bulbs have to go on for you. However you do it you've got to get rid of guilt.

GO DO IT

1. Take some time to describe, in as much detail as you can, the life you would like. Do it at the day/week/month and year level as we described above. Maybe make a first cut and then add to it as new things occur. Paint as complete a picture as you can. Make it a daydream that you return to – while you're stuck in traffic; during a boring meeting or while your plane is taxiing to the gate.

2. Make the list of people affected by your life and rate it as described above.

3. If you do feel guilty then get your hands on Mr Dyer's book. Alternatively, try to figure out for yourself why worrying – over past events that can't be changed or future events that may never happen – is completely and utterly pointless, a waste of time and energy and completely immobilising.

CHAPTER 15

Getting the Life You Want

In this chapter I describe two different ways to go about getting the life you want. I call the two methods 'plan your way to your new life' and 'live your way to your new life' respectively. Either or both of them will work in any situation. However, the first method would be particularly good if there was one overriding change you wanted to make in your life or some big 'thing' you wanted to achieve. Examples would be climbing Mount Everest, starting your own business, getting a new job, working a four-day week in your current job.

The second method would work best if:
- You were trying to do this for the first time, or
- You had been working towards your new life but then – for whatever reason – had drifted, strayed, fallen into old habits, and were trying to get back on the straight and narrow, or
- There was a difficult period coming up –at work, for example – and you wanted to make sure that you didn't lose the work/life balance you have.

Here they are.

Plan your way to your new life

Once you've figured out what kind of life you want, one way to achieve it is to build and execute a plan to get you there.

Just before we get into that though, a word of caution. You want to make sure you do the right plan, i.e. the one that solves the right problem. Let me give you an example. One of the case study people, in his initial email, said this: 'However, I have other goals that I can't seem to get time for... For the last 2 years, a friend and myself have been working on a website aimed at becoming a full-time endeavour. We have a working application, however, I can't put the time we need to make this successful.'

As we talked about this it became clear that the problem was not necessarily a problem to do with lack of time. The two people involved had, as they said, 'a working application', i.e. a piece of software that worked. However, they were spending much of their available time on improving the application. What they really should have been doing was spending the same amount of time *looking for customers*. If they then got to a point where they had customers and time was still a problem, then they could start to address that issue.

OK, so you need a plan. Of course you know how to do that if you've read Chapters 6 to 10. You may remember the plan for Green Cleaning Services that we developed. Here, once again, are the essentials of what you have to do. If you're already reasonably comfortable with the idea of building plans then this brief reminder should be enough for you. If not, it's probably best to go back and work your way through Chapters 6 to 10, building your plan as you go.

1. Decide a time horizon for your plan. If for example, you're starting a business then build a plan for no more than a year. In general, a shortish time horizon – six months, nine months, certainly not more than a year – will be better for you. It will keep you focused on getting some change in the short term. My own preference would be for a series of 90-day plans rather than one plan lasting a year. Sometimes politicians or new CEOs talk about 'the first hundred days'. In many ways it's a good way to think.

2. Decide exactly what you're trying to do. And remember what we said in Chapter 2 about goals having to be SMART (Specific, Measurable, Achievable, Realistic, Time-bound). One of my case studies started out with a goal 'to establish a group of active services and users that demonstrate that ACME as an application can attract and keep a user base'. Notice how different this is from what they ended up with – to reach 100,000 paid bookings per day.

3. Build the list of jobs. Identify the big blocks first. Then, for each big block, figure out all the detailed jobs, the chain or sequence of events that makes up each big block. Go back to Chapter 8 if you're in any

doubt about how to do this. See how we went about building the Green Cleaning Services plan. Use that approach and mindset to build your plan.

4. Once you've figured out the jobs, you can start to estimate (for each job):
   - Work – how much work in person-days or person-hours is in that job
   - Duration – how long the job will take
   - Dependencies – what jobs, if any, this job depends on and what jobs depend on it
   - Budget or cost – what the job will cost, both the labour and the other costs
   - Who's going to do it
   - What that person's availability is.

5. Make sure you put some contingency in the plan.

6. If your new life involves some change to your income stream or some threat to your income stream – e.g. if you're thinking of starting your own business – then it's best to represent your plan as a spreadsheet, i.e. showing what money gets spent when and what money gets earned when. You're going to have to watch this like a hawk if you are to stop yourself from getting into financial trouble.

7. Make sure you do a risk analysis (see Chapter 9) – again especially for plans involving a threat to your income stream, so that you don't get yourself into difficulties.

8. Once you have your basic plan, you can then start to do 'what-ifs' on it and look at alternative ways of getting things done. (See also the next section on taking risks.) Decide on the way that's going to work best for you.

9. Now start executing your plan as described in Chapter 10. Try to follow the plan as best you can. The plan will have identified and, in some cases, resolved problems you might otherwise have run into. It will have shown you what depends on what, what has to start when, what depends on other people. It will have identified the major things that could go wrong. If you start to do what the plan says – every day, every week – crossing off activities as they're done, you should start to make progress towards your new life.

On taking risks

You'll remember the plan for Green Cleaning Services deliberately chose a low-risk strategy. If you were to implement the plan that we came up with there, you could keep your day job while you explored whether Green Cleaning Services was a runner or not. You made less money that way – because you had to pay someone to do the work that you could have done – but you didn't end up doing anything that was potentially fatal to your income.

One could conceivably grow Green Cleaning Services into a multinational business that way – hiring, initially, a salesman and then further staff – without ever leaving your day job. That is – until you were a multi-millionaire and didn't really need the paltry salary they paid you any longer! That's one end of the spectrum.

On the other end would be to do what I did when I started my company – leaving my job with a month's salary having just arrived in the bank. I'm not recommending it. It's certainly not for the faint-hearted. It did have the virtue that failure was not an option – a condition which has a tendency to keep one very – and I mean, very – focused on the matter at hand.

Somewhere between these two ends of the spectrum you'll have to find your place. 'You can't make an omelette without breaking eggs' goes one old saying. And – one of my favourites – 'the man who never made a mistake never made anything'. The tools we've described, especially risk analysis, will help you to understand the risks. But at some stage you may just have to close your eyes and jump. The only question then is what the drop is. But risk analysis will enable you to choose a drop that you can cope with. It's a good tool. Use it often.

Live your way to your new life

Here's the second way you could go about starting to live the life you want to live. It incorporates some ideas we've seen previously, most notably the importance of having a daily routine, prioritising viciously, going home on time and the 40-hour week.

We're going to deal with things in the following order:

- Life – day-to-day stuff;
- Life – projects;
- Work – day-to-day stuff;
- Work – projects.

Here's what to do – and be sure you do it in exactly the order that it's given here. This will ensure that your life doesn't get squeezed out by your work.

Make your life list

No surprises here. Make a list of all the 'life' (i.e. non-work) stuff that you're involved in at the moment. (If you've got a list already, you can just extract the life (i.e. non-work) stuff from it.) You'll notice when you do this that the list has two types of things in it. There are one-off, 'project'-type things and there is day-to-day stuff.

For example, some projects that some of the case study people had were to 'put up a shed for a pony for the girls', or 'start my own business on the side', or 'I want to have the time and energy to tackle my photo collection at home – having thousands of digital photos of the kids that never see the light of day is ridiculous'. Then there is day-to-day stuff – things like (again from the case study people):

- I don't want to have to bring work home
- I want to keep up my exercise regime
- I want to give my wife the time she wants to go walking in the evenings
- I want to spend more time with my family
- I want to spend more time with my wife.

Divide your list into the projects and the day-to-day stuff. Now, let's look at the day-to-day stuff first.

Life day-to-day stuff

1. Prioritise your list using the 'if I could only do one thing on this list, what would it be' technique.
2. Now make a daily schedule that you're going to follow each *week* day (i.e. Monday to Friday) where you fit the things from your day-to-day list into your schedule. (I know this may sound a bit over the top but it really is the only way you can ensure that these things will happen.) Fit them into your schedule in priority order, i.e. fit the most important

one first and the next most important and the next most important and so on. Most importantly, assume that you will leave work at normal finishing time. Thus, when you have done this, your list might look like this:

07:00–08:00	Exercise
09:00–17:00	Do my day job
17:00–19:00	Go home; eat; spend time with family
19:00–20:00	More time with family while wife walks
20:00–21:00	Do garden and outside jobs.

3. If there are things that are on your list that haven't made it into the daily schedule then you have a few possibilities:

    • Get up earlier or go to bed later and so make the day longer, i.e. make more time available

    • Shorten your time spent at work. (Why not? Shorter lunch break. Be more efficient using some of the other ideas in this book. Don't waste your time or let other people waste it.)

    • Change the priority of things on your life day-to-day list so that you can fit them into your day

    • Forget about these things on your life day-to-day list for the moment.

4. Now begin to follow this schedule on a day-to-day basis for Monday through Friday. Do this until it becomes a habit.

> **GO DO IT**
>
> **Sort out your life day-to-day stuff as we just described.**

Life projects

You still have to get your life projects done, so how are you going to do that? Well, first you need to prioritise them, using the 'if I could only do one thing what would it be technique'. Then you need to (a) figure out how much of your time they're going to take up, and then (b) find time to do them. To do the former you need to build a plan and figure out how much work (not duration) your project will require. To do the latter you then need to find time either in your Monday to Friday schedule or else at the weekend.

Some of your projects may be small and fairly self-contained. For example, the shed for the pony mentioned above may be a weekend's work for somebody who knows what they're doing. But other projects, like the 'start my own business on the side' project mentioned above, may require a lot more than that. Then you would have to do a plan along the lines of the Green Cleaning Services plan that we did in Part Two. Of all the benefits we've already mentioned of doing this, perhaps the principle one will be that you spend the limited amount of time you have wisely. Once you've built the plan, you will then know the sequence of little jobs that have to be done and you can start to find time for them either during the weekdays or at the weekend.

GO DO IT

1. Prioritise your life projects list.

2. Starting with the highest priority one, and working your way down the list, do the following:

   Find a place for small projects in your diary.

   Build a plan for large projects as described in Part Two. This will give the sequence of events that you must follow. Now, beginning with the first job, find a place for it in your diary. Then the next, then the next and so on. Now your projects are rolling.

Now we're ready to look at your work stuff. Notice that if you approach things this way, the problem you're now trying to solve is how to fit everything into your working day. You already have your time outside work – your life – scheduled and safe. Now you're going to do the same for your work. This is as it should be.

Make your work list

Now make your work list. Write down all of the things you have on at work just now. Have two categories – day-to-day stuff and projects. (If you already have a list then just extract the work stuff.)

Work day-to-day stuff

1. Prioritise the day-to-day part of your list using the 'if I could only do one thing on this list, what would it be' technique.
2. Now, taking the items on this list in priority order, fit them into your weekly schedule (diary). Some for example, checking emails, will have to be done every day or maybe a couple of times a day. Some, such as 'the Monday meeting', will belong on certain days.
3. If, when you've done this, your diary's more than full, i.e. you already have too much work to do – even before projects are taken into account – then you need to go and talk to your boss. I suggest you do a Dance Card (see Chapter 3) and have proposals for him/her as to what you'd like done. (While I've never liked the boss-ism, 'Don't bring me problems, bring me solutions', I think it's more sensible for you to propose the solutions than for them to do so. If only because you're more likely to get a solution that's good for you.) What choices do you have/what options can you offer? Well, they're pretty simple really:
   • Delay certain things
   • Drop certain things
   • Change priorities
   • Give things to somebody else/get somebody to help you.
   And if he won't go with any of those, you need to point out that, because demand is greater than supply, then:
   • There are going to be delays
   • And some things won't get done
   • And that some things won't be able to be done properly or as well as they might have been.

GO DO IT

Sort out your work day-to-day stuff as we just described.

Finally then, you must turn your attention to your work projects.

Work projects

As before you need to prioritise your work projects using the 'if I could only do one thing what would it be' technique. Then you need to (a) figure out how much of your time they're going to take up, and then (b) find time to do them. To do the former you need to build a plan and figure out how much work (not duration) your project will require. To do the latter you then need to find time in your weekly schedule.

Some of your projects may be small and fairly self-contained and can be slotted easily into your weekly schedule. But others may require a lot more than that. Do a plan. Then, once you've built the plan, you will then know the sequence of little jobs that have to be done and you can start to find time for them in your weekly schedule.

GO DO IT

1. Prioritise your work projects list.

2. Starting with the highest priority one, and working your way down the list, do the following:

   Find a place for small projects in your weekly schedule.

   Build a plan for large projects as described in Chapter 8. This will give the sequence of events that you must follow. Now, beginning with the first job, find a place for it in your weekly schedule. Then the next, then the next and so on. Now your projects are rolling.

Now use the following 30-day calendar to follow your routine for the next 30 days. Photocopy this and mark off each day where you complete your new routine as planned. If you falter, never mind, just go back to the beginning and start again. You want to get 30 days in a row. By then your new routine should have become a habit.

30-DAY CALENDAR

1	2	3	4
Follow your new routine and mark today off if you were successful in following it as planned.	Follow your new routine and mark today off if you were successful in following it as planned.	Follow your new routine and mark today off if you were successful in following it as planned.	Follow your new routine and mark today off if you were successful in following it as planned.
8	**9**	**10**	**11**
Follow your new routine and mark today off if you were successful in following it as planned.	Follow your new routine and mark today off if you were successful in following it as planned.	Follow your new routine and mark today off if you were successful in following it as planned.	Follow your new routine and mark today off if you were successful in following it as planned.
15	**16**	**17**	**18**
Follow your new routine and mark today off if you were successful in following it as planned.	Follow your new routine and mark today off if you were successful in following it as planned.	Follow your new routine and mark today off if you were successful in following it as planned.	Follow your new routine and mark today off if you were successful in following it as planned.
22	**23**	**24**	**25**
Follow your new routine and mark today off if you were successful in following it as planned.	Follow your new routine and mark today off if you were successful in following it as planned.	Follow your new routine and mark today off if you were successful in following it as planned.	Follow your new routine and mark today off if you were successful in following it as planned.
29	**30**		
Follow your new routine and mark today off if you were successful in following it as planned.	Follow your new routine and mark today off if you were successful in following it as planned.		

5	6	7
Follow your new routine and mark today off if you were successful in following it as planned.	Follow your new routine and mark today off if you were successful in following it as planned.	Follow your new routine and mark today off if you were successful in following it as planned.
12	**13**	**14**
Follow your new routine and mark today off if you were successful in following it as planned.	Follow your new routine and mark today off if you were successful in following it as planned.	Follow your new routine and mark today off if you were successful in following it as planned.
19	**20**	**21**
Follow your new routine and mark today off if you were successful in following it as planned.	Follow your new routine and mark today off if you were successful in following it as planned.	Follow your new routine and mark today off if you were successful in following it as planned.
26	**27**	**28**
Follow your new routine and mark today off if you were successful in following it as planned.	Follow your new routine and mark today off if you were successful in following it as planned.	Follow your new routine and mark today off if you were successful in following it as planned.

This stuff works

If you do as we've described then your new life will start to take shape before your eyes. The more you follow your new routine, the more successful you will be. This has very much been my experience. Conversely, the more I have drifted back to my old ways – by which I mean my old priorities – the more I have found myself stuck in a life and a daily routine that I don't particularly like or want.

This hasn't just been my experience. Here are a couple of eminent men on the same subject. First the American philosopher Henry David Thoreau (*Walden*, 1854):

> *If one advances confidently in the direction of his own dreams, and endeavours to live the life which he has imagined, he will meet with a success unexpected in common hours.*

And here is another that is usually attributed to philosopher Johann Wolfgang Von Goethe (though for the correct attribution, see www.goethesociety.org/pages/quotescom.html):

> *Until one is committed there is hesitancy, the chance to draw back, always ineffectiveness. Concerning all acts of initiation and creation there is one elementary truth the ignorance of which kills countless ideas and splendid plans: that the moment one definitely commits oneself, then providence moves too. All sorts of things occur to help that would never have otherwise occurred. A whole stream of events issue from the decision, raising in ones favour all manner of unforeseen incidents, meetings and material assistance which no man could have dreamed would have come his way. What you can do or dream, begin it. Boldness has genius, power and magic in it. Begin it now.*

All that work you did in the previous chapter, imagining what your new life would be like – here now is the chance to live it. That daily routine that you sketched out in such detail, start to live that routine today.

You may remember my own routine that I described in Chapter 14:

1. 1 hour's writing
2. *On Becoming A Novelist*
3. ETP
4. 2,000 words
5. Exercise
6. Music

I said that that was how I would like to spend my day. This was not strictly true. In a perfect world, if I were writing all the time, then this is how I would want to spend my day:

1. 1 hour's writing
2. *On Becoming A Novelist*
3. 2,000 words
4. Exercise
5. Music

In a perfect world, writing would be my day job. That's not the case at the moment but the difference between my ideal day and the day I actually live is narrowing – just as Thoreau said it would. Now it's true that I still have to go on the road to do my day job, but the number of days I do that is also going down. In the first half of this year it was ten days down on last year. If that were to follow through to the end of the year, then that would be twenty days closer to the ideal life.

You see – this stuff works!

PART FIVE: CASE STUDIES

There are four case studies. I worked with a lot more than four people and some of their stories are woven into the text and aspects of their experience have been used to make points there. I felt there was limited value in lining up a small army of people to say, 'I tried it and it worked'. The best way for you to verify whether *Work Less, Achieve More* works is to try it yourself. Then you'll see that it does.

A large number of people wanted to start something new – in most cases, their own businesses. Rather than relate their stories, the case study of Green Cleaning Services in Part Two describes how to go about building a plan to get a business off the ground. In addition, the examples given in Part Three are derived from having done supply-and-demand work a number of times. (The names have been changed to protect the innocent!)

All of the case studies describe people who made major changes to their lives – the subject of Part Four.

Chapter 16 has one case study while Chapter 17 describes three.

CHAPTER 16

Case Study No. 1

Working less and achieving more doesn't require complex or difficult ideas. All it requires is a bit of thought and then the guts to actually take some decisions, make some changes and make those changes permanent.

This first case study shows how an incredibly simple idea can make a profound change to someone's life. It is a truly inspiring story. This one has been written so as to preserve the person's privacy. The person works in IT. The next section is – almost verbatim – the email which he sent to me.

The case study

If I understand the subject matter correctly I think the book is a great idea. I have jotted a few thoughts... If your book helps one person to get off the hamster's wheel it will be worth it. It is a horrible place to be stuck. I know there are hundreds of stories like mine.

Some of this is personal but it is needed to underline how close to the edge I think I was. I was very stressed. Working less has made a massive difference and there is no doubt it outweighs the financial loss. I should have done it earlier in my life. I now work less and achieve more as life is not all about work.

Who do you work for? For 15 years I said that I worked for my employer; now I say I work for 'myself' or 'family and friends'. This is the only life I will get - as far as I know. Why in God's name would I work for anyone else?

Question: Are you in the back seat of a cab in a foreign country where you don't know the city and the driver does not speak your language and you have just seen that monument for the third time or are you doing the driving with the latest road map that's available?

Answer: You should 'Drive your own life'. There is nothing worse than being dragged from one unplanned situation to another when you don't even have the time to realise it.

Peace increase
Taking control of any situation leads to reduced stress. One cannot and would not want to control everything in your life but peace can come from saying I gave that my best shot and I really don't think I could do any more to make the situation better. I use the word peace in the sense of peace of mind. By this I mean that you

can allow your mind to relax and not have your to-do list buzzing around non-stop. When you lack peace of mind you can do nothing comfortably. I make this comment in relation to work and private life. I was in a situation that I literally could not sit down in the evening for more than 15 minutes – I had to be doing something or at least subconsciously I felt I had to.

Needless to say I nearly drove myself and those closest to me mad.

More control equals less stress as you can say to yourself I have planned for this or if I haven't I have the time to do so.

My experience and the need for change
Over the last ten years I have found myself in the following situation:
- 10 years ago Father (still going strong) had massive stroke 2 weeks before my wedding – leaves him hemiplegic and with no speech
- Get married – postpone honeymoon
- Brother (I have one brother) has first child – son is autistic (this takes a lot of his time). He has two more kids over the following 7 years
- Father in intensive rehab for 6 months
- Father moves home to live with mother for 2.5 years
- Mother finds it extremely difficult to cope
- Father-in-law dies suddenly (obvious issues for my wife – they were very close)
- I continue to work like mad
- Find home for father – lengthy difficult process with health authorities and politicians
- Mother has stroke leaving her with no short-term memory
- Wife becomes pregnant
- I continue to work like mad
- Visiting both parents in different homes
- Son is born
- Wife goes back to work full-time
- NEARLY GO MAD myself
- Mother dies after 3 years in home
- I continue to work like mad
- Wife has our second child
- My wife and I change to 4-day week each (I don't do Thursdays and she doesn't do Fridays. (She takes half of Friday on Parental Leave and gets paid 4.5 days a week)
- My life changes completely – back to the sanity I once had.

I had to change. I should have done it sooner
The wake-up call happened one day when my brother said to me that if he was to suffer the same fate as our father at the same age he did (this is not impossible – he was very fit, non-smoker, drank little, active mind, not overweight, regular check-ups) because of hereditary issues his life was more than half over. This stunned me.

4-day week
Project work particularly lends itself to this arrangement, i.e. you can plan for it. Typically project managers get this idea. Others types of people may need more convincing. Work can be teed up for consideration by others on your day off – it is rare that I find I miss a meeting that I really wanted to be at as they are not meetings I have arranged! Over the life of a project work gets the benefit as there

is no way I do 20 % less than the others on the project. It's probably good that there are 'core days' - when everybody has to be in the office - as it can be a bit of a nuisance if people need to meet to make decisions and are not in the office at the same time.

Benefits

- Kids (aged 4 and 2) are at home for the majority of the week. Huge psychological benefit as neither of us liked them in crèche 5 days a week
- Our days off can be used to get stuff done when it is not so busy - stuff that would have to be done at the weekend otherwise. For example:
  - Doctors visits
  - Visit family, grandparents or cousins
  - Recycling - bring the kids and teach them
  - Gardening - kids love it. Teaches them about growing stuff, etc.
- The kids do everything you do on a Thursday and it is interesting for them. e.g. Dentist/passport applications/leaving the car to the mechanic/going into town for specific items/shopping, etc.
- Doing some things on a Thursday is a lot easier than let's say a Saturday. Cinema, playgrounds, swimming pools, day trips with the kids for example. The cinema is a good metaphor - why do I have to be forced to have my quality time at the time the rat race dictates. Rat race-free time is not free time. It's like exercise time in a prison. I was going to the beach on Saturday with the kids and the road was jammed with cars. It was going to take over 80 minutes to get there and back. I turned around and said 'let's go next Thursday'.
- The cinema on a Thursday is a little like living in the country - no traffic jams, not overcrowded, no queues, an easier pace. This makes me feel good as I am taking charge and not being dictated to.
- The weekends are as much mine now as they are the kids'. Their weekend starts on Wednesday evening and finishes on Sunday night.
- I can plan to do stuff that I want to do. Before, with two parents working, needing time for family, kids, house maintenance, random mandatory tasks, I was not getting to do all the things I needed to do, never mind getting to do anything that I alone wanted to do. Now I play golf, go watch football matches, do things on my own, etc. People wonder how I get the time do it.
- Over the last few years my wife and I have both been able to take trips abroad with our friends independently of each other. I know this would not be possible unless we felt we had enough in the tank to deal with a busy spell of 5-6 or 10 days when we were managing on our own. I have been in Africa twice and South America playing golf and my wife goes to Spain on sun holidays or New York. This is not boasting but I want to emphasise this would not happen if we were stressed to our gills - we would say no to each other.
- Very roughly, on 60k a year I lose about 120 euro a week. That is 12k less 50% for tax divided by 12 divided by 4.3. Find another way to reduce your costs (have no landline phone for example) for, let's say, half of it and get a pay rise for half of the remaining balance (work will accommodate a minor rise like this - 3k). This means you need to go without 30 quid a week. This is not too difficult.

How to organise it?

My story is that I applied for Parental Leave and was not answered so I made a decision because of no reply. HR felt obliged then I think to offer 4-day week as I had sent them a mail saying if you don't reply by such a date I am taking this as approval. I then went and booked the crèche for Monday to Wednesday only for the year.

Contract regarding redundancy should be considered, i.e. one should factor in length of full-time service when calculating a 'week's work'.

Annual leave is reduced by a fifth but the need for days off is hugely reduced and when the bank holidays come along you are sucking diesel as there [are] lots of days out of the office.

Analysis

There is not a lot I want to add to this except to point out how two of our three simple ideas were employed here to devastating effect.

Prioritise viciously

First, the author decided where work came in his scheme of priorities. Sure, the need to earn a living and support his dependants was important, just as it is for all of us. But there were other priorities as well – peace of mind, the ability to relax and have a better quality of life and spend time on the things that really mattered and with the people who really mattered.

Say 'no' nicely

After that it was just a question of saying 'no' to a five-day week. That was it. And notice that it was just one occurrence of saying 'no'. It didn't have to be done constantly or repeatedly or every day. Just once and then that was it – straight into a new life.

CHAPTER 17

Case Study No. 2

This second case study is made up of three different people who all started out with similar problems. Again you'll be able to see how our three simple ideas improved things for them. For reasons of anonymity, I have called two of these people Anne and Claire. Anne works in a job while Claire is self-employed. The third person is called Ciara and works freelance. Here are the positions that these three people started from in their own words.

Where they started

Anne

We have 2 children (5 and 6yrs old) ... and we both work full-time ... I am just frustrated that I have to work 5 days a week so I never have the headspace to do all the other things on my eternal 'To Do' list because I spend any spare time I have doing overtime at home, cooking, cleaning, grocery shopping, organising kids' birthday parties, taking the kids to activities, etc. etc. I never have time to read a newspaper, never mind a book. I watch very little TV. I know I should spend more quality time with kids. Luckily I have a very good childminder and finally succumbed to hiring someone to do the ironing. I dream of being able to organise the thousands of photos and hours of video clips I have of [the] kids some day. At least I get to exercise 3/4 times a week. Without that I'd have gone insane long ago.

Ciara

I work freelance so tend to be involved with many diverse projects at a time. Here's a rough outline - this varies depending on term times:
- *Lecturing/module administration, undergrad and postgrad at a university*
- *3 days at another organisation on numerous projects*
- *Saturday morning - Speech and Drama teaching (3 classes)*
- *Saturday afternoon - class (studying for teaching diploma)*
- *Freelance research/design of educational resources (on and off during the year)*
- *Delivery of film archive presentations (evenings/daytimes on and off)*
- *Voluntary work - ChildLine (and occasionally with the Youth Empowerment Scheme)*

I'm also connected to a small start-up training organisation - I and a colleague received start-up funds and business advice from an enterprise scheme. We start our first contract providing civic leadership training in October and have also applied for another tender for youth workshops. There are only two of us working on this and we would both really like to make more time to develop workshop templates and try to source business. (This is what I'd really like to concentrate on.)

I tend to do a lot of 'work more hours' particularly when preparing for lectures. Last semester I ended up working really late into the night and had very early starts in the morning. I still however felt dreadfully unprepared for lectures which had a knock-on effect on my delivery etc. My boyfriend is a freelance musician and record producer which means he has a really unusual schedule - and often it's difficult for us to find free time! My three closest friends live in London, Manchester and Spain so it's tough trying to fit in time to see them, both to visit and also when they are home. This semester I will be teaching a couple of undergrad modules and one postgrad module - so I will have a major amount of reading each week. Because of where I live there's a fair bit of travelling to factor in as well. I'd like to feel a bit more confident about delivery of lectures but somehow try to limit the preparation time as well. I'd also, by this time next year, really like to be working at least half time on building up the business I'm working on.

Claire

I am currently a freelance science communication consultant. That means that I talk about science to people (in schools, at science festivals and more recently on TV) and research science education and people's opinions about science. I first started struggling with work/life balance when I was doing my PhD, and trying to run a schools education company and do consultancy work on the side. I have always struggled with this, and improved somewhat earlier this year when I made the decision to stop working from home and to move into a shared office space. I now want to grow my business and take on my first employee later on this year. I also want to relaunch my company with a new name and start advertising. At the moment I don't even have a website - it's just one of those things I never got around to - I get all my work from word of mouth. I work on up to about 12 projects simultaneously and feel like there is always something slipping and that the list never ends. I really need to think strategically about expanding my company but feel like I never have time. I travel lots for work and am always up and down the country for meetings, workshops and conferences, often abroad too. This week was typical in getting back from a conference late Saturday night, Sunday in London, Monday in Liverpool, Tues office, Weds in a school all day in Essex, Thurs Manchester, Fri a different school in Essex, this week is similar with Liverpool-Edinburgh-Liverpool. If I want to grow my business I need to stop chasing my tail and start being more strategic - but I don't know how. Help!!

What they did

What all three women did was the following:

1. They looked ahead a certain period of time and made a list of all the things they had to do during that period.

2. They quantified how much work was involved in each of these things.
3. They prioritised the list. Some went straight for 'if I could only do one thing on this list what would it be?' others did the 'wildly important' (or not) thing first.
4. They started spending more time on the top priorities.
5. They spent less (or no) time on the stuff near the bottom of the list. This was done by ignoring stuff, letting stuff go hang, not doing stuff or – in Anne's case – getting their boss to take stuff away from them.

The results

Anne

As a matter of fact, home life has improved significantly in the last few weeks. I find myself reading newspapers again, playing games with the kids and having time to go clothes shopping!

Ciara

Things are going great – I have to say I'm much calmer about the semester ahead now I've done some proper planning! I'm going to have a go now at the same exercise for next year. This has really helped clarify the next few months for me which has been a great help.

This process has been extremely helpful. I am already spending my time more efficiently, enjoying my work more and feel calmer and less anxious generally. As a result I am more confident and feel that the quality of my work has improved. I revise my project planning regularly and this in itself is a therapeutic exercise. This has been a real turning point.

Claire

I think what I have really learned from this process so far is to be realistic about how long things are going to take me, which has really helped me be less stressed. For example, last week I was really up against it one day trying to get too much stuff finished. The report that I was going to start writing at 8 p.m. last Thursday was for a client that has messed me around a lot for the last year and that I'm not too bothered about working for again. I also had a report to finish the following day for another client that I really enjoy working with and who really appreciates my work. So I decided that instead of doing an average job of both reports in a rush, I would meet the deadline for my better client and put the others off for a couple of weeks, when I would next have a window of time to realistically complete the work for them. My husband was very pleased that I came home from the office at a reasonable time to enjoy a nice meal with him, instead of working until stupid o'clock and making myself ill. I then got into work feeling fresh on Friday morning and had finished my other report before lunch. Cue happy and stress-free weekend.

The list has been a tremendous help and I am still using it every day. Moving

WORK LESS, ACHIEVE MORE

*from my previous system of having a daily list (always with more on it than I could
ever get finished) to just one list organised in order of priority was scary at first,
but liberating. I didn't realise how much the sense of failure of never achieving
what I set myself during the day was getting me down – even if I had achieved
loads, if I didn't tick everything off I felt bad. Now I just get through what I can
from the top of the list then go home. A much better idea! And certainly
something that I think I will use when my employee comes on board to monitor
what they are doing and their list of priorities. What the list has also done is help
me identify the things I'm good at getting done quickly and the stuff that tends to
languish at the bottom.*

*I think what I have learned is to be realistic and understand how long things will
take me. This has helped me set realistic deadlines and avoid getting stressed out
in the first place.*

*I'm now excited about coming to work in the morning and no longer have the
feeling that things are slipping away from me, so I feel much more in control. This
has made me more motivated and I also have a lot more energy, I seem to need
less sleep and am making more of my evenings and weekends. I guess it's the kind
of thing where you don't realise how much the constant low-level worry is getting
to you. I really have got my life back so THANK YOU!*

Fergus O'Connell offers one-to-one coaching in applying *Work Less, Achieve More* to your work or to your life. The coaching is done by email and by phone and a limited number of places is available every year. If you would like to find out more, you can email him at fergus.oconnell@etpint.com using the title line 'Coaching'.

Fergus's company ETP (www.etpint.com) provides consultancy for organisations wishing to implement the ideas described in Part Three. It also offers training courses in *Work Less, Achieve More* that are run publicly and can also be run in-house. For more information or with any feedback on this book, please email Fergus as above.

Bibliography

Allen, David (2002) *Getting Things Done*, London: Piatkus Books

Bolles, Richard Nelson (2007) *What Colour Is Your Parachute?* Berkeley, California: Ten Speed Press

Brooks, Frederick P. (1995) *The Mythical Man Month and Other Essays on Software Engineering*, New York: Addison Wesley

Covey, Stephen R. (2005) *The 4 Disciplines of Execution*, Salt Lake City: FranklinCovey

DeMarco, Tom (1997) *The Deadline*, New York: Dorset House Publishing

Dyer, Wayne W. (1998) *Your Erroneous Zones*, London: Time Warner Paperbacks

Thoreau, Henry David (2006) *Walden*, London: Everyman's Library

Index

Note: Page numbers in *italic* denote references in the cleaning business example or case studies. Page numbers in **bold** denote larger sections.